From Dark *to* Light

Geneva S. Rivers

Inks and Bindings
888-290-5218
www.inksandbindings.com
orders@inksandbindings.com

TABLE OF CONTENTS

From Dark to Light

Not day and night, dark and light, but a lifestyle, one of righteousness and the other of that which is contrary. Not the going down of the sun, but the uprising of a new life, a life not contrary to the will of God. There was a time in history called the Dark Ages, when things weren't going well from the natural perspective. And now we dwell in an age of disparity, a spiritual dark age, a life separated from God. The availability is here, but the accepting is not. We see it each day, and the change that is needful can come only through God. This is not a matter the Act of Congress can mend. Only the receiving of God, even from the beginning of creation, for all things were made for man's purpose.

God supplied the needs of man before man existed. He spoke the world into being, yet when it came to man, he formed him with his own hands. In this it was established that the two should coincide—creator and creature—agreeing, having the same view, and walking in fellowship.

But Satan came in with an offer that should have been refused. Men say the violence of our time is the fruit of emotional disorder, yet more certainly it is the lack of a God-ordained life. For the scripture says there is nothing broken that God cannot heal. I say again, the Act of Congress cannot fix world conditions when men don't stay in the perspective of their created purpose. A world that once knew no sin became a world of sin. And the only solution is to return to that purpose for which man was made: to honor God and to love one another. Righteousness bringeth life; sin bringeth death, even separation from God. The breath in man's body is not the whole of life. To be complete, God must be within. Apart from him, man finds himself in snares that harm both himself and others. Look around at the world this day, and ye know it is not the plan of God, for God is love.

To pass from darkness into light is to forsake the ungodly way. This is not for self alone but for the good of others as well. We were created with purpose: to worship God and to be fruitful toward one another. To be fruitful is to be of benefit each to his brother. When asked of Cain, *"Where is thy brother Abel?"* Cain answered, *"Am I my brother's keeper?"* If we but saw each other as keepers of the brethren, much of the evil in this world would vanish away.

To be examples of righteousness, void of that which is wrong, what joy would fill the earth! Even as we desire peace for ourselves, we must seek it for others. And if any desire it not, then let us search our own hearts and fashion a new thought pattern, for all that God made was good. To return unto the original will bring world change. It may not blot out the evil that hath been, yet it becometh a building stone for the new.

The things I used to do, I do them no more. Confession and turning bring a cleansing of the heart. Purity, dignity, and respect follow after, and honor is restored. For man was not created for the flesh alone. There is also the spiritual, which cannot mend the world's brokenness. Man abideth not in the purpose for which he was made, and thus a world that knew no sin became a world filled with sin. We see the fruit daily. Some believeth the violence of our time is the fruit of a madness, yet more surely it is due to the lack of a God-ordained life. For the act of man toward God is forgotten, though he alone hath power to keep one's mind in perfect peace. God made not mankind complete in himself but left a space for himself, a place for divine fellowships. When the chain is broken, love waxeth cold. That which restraineth man from doing contrary to God's will is absent, and the result is what we behold in these days. The more lives ordained of the Lord, the less violence shall abound, and every man should desire this for himself.

And if the world changes not, yet I need not be the cause thereof. If each man hast his mind, surely there would be change for the better. Therefore, let us go unto the word of God, and therein find what is necessary to heal our estate. From the first man, Adam, who kept not the command of God, came disobedience. After the work of creation was finished, God beheld all he had made—male and female—and said, *"It is very good."* Yet man left it not so. He was given much to enjoy and only one thing forbidden, but that he coveted. Thus did man become as dross, the worthless part cast aside, for outside the will of God man becometh vain. Yet he was made for worship, and therein alone is his completeness. Without this, man is undone and falleth into that which is contrary to God. In his word are the *"shalt dos"* and the *"shalt nots."* Let us hear them and be wise.

Perhaps I should speak of my own conversion. While I lay in the hospital, awaiting surgery, I said unto the Lord: *"If I live, I will truly live."*

When I was discharged, the doctor warned me, *"No bending or stooping."* With a husband and three darling children and a sewing shop to tend, I went home. Yet within me stirred a thought: there is more to life than this. I bowed upon my knees and prayed, *"Lord, if you don't want me, I don't want me either."* And I spoke many other words, desiring to be right with him. I remembered the doctor's command: no bending or stooping. So I decided to lie on the bed for a while. Then a change came over me. It was as though I were lifted out of one person into another, to the point that I found myself feeling the bed to see if the old me remained. When I returned to the doctor for my checkup, he said I was completely healed.

"I have never seen anything like this before," quoth he. This was a miracle.

Ways and means are not for the economy only but for the soul also. For the person I am today is not the person I once was.

Topic: "All People is God People"

Exodus 15:26 (KJV)

[26] And said, if thou wilt diligently hearken to the voice of the LORD, thy God, and wilt do that which is right in his sight, and wilt give ear to his commandments, and keep all his statutes, I will put none of these diseases upon thee, which I have brought upon the Egyptians: for I am the LORD that healeth thee.

2 Chronicles 7:14

[14] If my people, which are called by my name, shall humble themselves, and pray, and seek my face, and turn from their wicked ways; then will I hear from heaven, and will forgive their sin, and will heal their land.

Isaiah 53:5

[5] But he was wounded for our transgressions, he was bruised for our iniquities: the chastisement of our peace was upon him; and with his stripes we are healed.

Ephesians 2:11-12

[11] Wherefore remember, that ye being in time past, Gentiles in the flesh, who are called Uncircumcision by that which is called the Circumcision in the flesh made by hands; [12] that at that time ye were without Christ, being aliens from the

commonwealth of Israel, and strangers from the covenants of promise, having no hope, and without God in the world:

Using the subject, "*All People Are God's People.*" There's a saying: for every action there is a reaction. Today's message is of man's action and God's reaction and the feedback of them both. And this venture is not for a chosen few only but for the whole wide world, for all people are God's people. Even among the descendants of Abraham, chosen to be a people unto God, there were strangers among them who became part of that movement. The conditions and promises required then are still required in today's time. For that which he said, "Be still and know that I am God. I am the Lord; I change not." Therefore, the change must come from the side of man. But he is a God of opportunity, giving unto all mankind the offer to open the doors of their hearts, that he may enter therein.

Hear then what was spoken in Exodus 15:26: "*If thou wilt diligently hearken to the voice of the LORD thy God, and wilt do that which is right in his sight, and wilt give ear to his commandments, and keep all his statutes, I will put none of these diseases upon thee, which I have brought upon the Egyptians: for I am the LORD that healeth thee.*" This word is not just for the Jews only, but for all nations—a worldwide movement. Let us consider if more people lived by the standard, "*Greater is He that is in me, than he that is in the world.*" For God also said, "I will put none of these diseases upon thee." We need not wait for the city in the sky to know a better day; we can taste it now. For if more men and women lived God-fearing lives, though this would now remove the Day of Judgement, yet it would be a guarantee to be standing on the right hand of God.

For the Scripture tells us that when the Son of Man shall come in his glory, and all the holy angels with him, then shall he sit upon the throne of his glory. Before him shall be gathered all nations, and he shall separate them one from another, as a shepherd divideth the sheep from the goats. God's resolve is not like that of man, for man saith that the majority rules. He shall set the sheep, those that served him, upon his right hand, but the goats, those that served Mammon, upon his left. Not that they didn't have the opportunity to become sheep, but they refused the Word of God.

Some say in certain countries, men cannot serve God openly, but serving beginneth in the heart. For God hath said, *"So shall my Word be that goeth forth out of my mouth: it shall not return unto me void, but it shall accomplish that which I please, and it shall prosper in the thing whereto I sent it."* Consider Ezra and Nehemiah, how God uses ungodly kings to fulfill his purpose. Remember how Jesus said unto Pilate, *"Thou couldest have no power at all against me, except it were given thee from above."* Forget not Jonah, to whom the Lord said, *"Arise, go to Nineveh, that great city, and cry against it; for their wickedness is come up before me."* And the king of that city arose from his throne, laid his robe aside, covered himself with sackcloth, and sat in ashes. What a witness that no power is greater than the power of God.

If Samson, with the jawbone of an ass, slew a thousand men, let us then consider what change may come when the people of God are in one accord, moving in the power of God. For the promise is not of health only but of restoration. Hear 2 Chronicles 7:14: *"If my people, which are called by my name, shall humble themselves, and pray, and seek my face, and turn from their wicked ways, then will I hear from heaven, and will forgive their sin, and will heal their land."* What a combination: unity of heart and mind toward God. For Jesus said, *"Where two or three are gathered in my name, there am I in the midst of them."* What then would be the outcome if multitudes were gathered?

As once he came down to confound those who said, *"Let us build us a city and a tower whose top may reach unto heaven,* and let us make us a name," so he also said unto Moses, "*I have surely seen the affliction of my people who are in Egypt, and have heard their cry by reason of their taskmasters, for I know their sorrows. And I have come down to deliver them out of the hand of the Egyptians and to bring them up out of that land unto a good land and a large one, unto a land flowing with milk and honey.*" Surely he shall be among his people when they are on the move for God. For he said, "*Lo, I am with you always, even unto the end of the world.*"

There's a saying that a loser cannot win, and a winner cannot lose. There is no losing for those that are on the right hand of God. For the right hand of God doesn't begin on Judgment Day, but even now, in this earthly life, when we commit ourselves unto Him. Paul said, "*I am ready to be offered, and the time of my departure is at hand. I have fought a good fight, I have finished my course, I have kept the faith.*" We know our birthdate, but no man knows his death date. Therefore, remain in a ready state. As was said, we can't always be "getting ready," but we must be ready. For no man knows the day nor the hour when the Lord shall come for His church without a spot or wrinkle.

Hear Isaiah 55:5: "*Behold, thou shalt call a nation that thou knowest not, and nations that knew not thee shall run unto thee, because of the Lord thy God and for the Holy One of Israel; for he hath glorified thee.*" All people are God's people. That which is meant for one is meant for all. If more would accept the invitation, what would the world be like? Think on these things: whatsoever things are true, whatsoever things are honest, whatsoever things are just, whatsoever things are pure, whatsoever things are lovely, whatsoever things are of good report, if there be any virtue, if there be any praise, think on these things. For in these things is the renewing of the mind and the putting away of the carnal mind, which cannot please God.

"Let this mind be in you, which was also in Christ Jesus." For he said, *"The son can do nothing of himself but what he seeth the father do. There is a song that saith, 'I want to be like Jesus.'"* Yet it is not only to be but also to do as Jesus did. For if more people sought to be like him, a better day would begin even now.

Wherefore remember, as Ephesians says, that ye being in time past Gentiles in the flesh, called uncircumcision by that which is called the circumcision in the flesh made by hands. But he is a Christian who is one inwardly, not in a mouth of words only, but in the circumcision of the heart, in the spirit, not in the letter, whose praise is not of men but of God. Anything that is without inner transformation is but pretense, able to deceive man but not God.

For we were once without Christ, aliens from the commonwealth of Israel, strangers from the covenants of promise, having no hope, and without God in the world. But that time is no more. For at forty and two generations, God the Spirit planted himself in the womb of the virgin Mary. She was found with the child of the Holy Ghost. Thus God the Spirit was made flesh, not for the Jews only, but for whosoever will. Red, yellow, black, and white—all are precious in His sight. For God sent not his son into the world to condemn the world, but that the world through him might be saved.

Therefore, if God is on the move for us, let us be on the move for him. For Jesus said, *"Ye are the salt of the earth: but if the salt have lost its flavor, wherewith shall it be salted?"* Salt is good, but if it loses its saltiness, it is good for nothing. For it were better not to have known the way of righteousness than to turn aside from it. A Christian's life is a gateway to the world, and if the light is put out, it affects not only that soul but all those who once beheld God's work in him. Therefore, he said, *"Let your light so shine before men, that they may see your good works, and glorify your Father which is in heaven."*

This message is about the people of God being on the move for God. And the result? Better days, even now. When hearts turn from ways contrary to the will of God, the impact of evil lessens. *"Greater is he that is in me than he that is in the world."* Remember the woman at the well. When she found out who Jesus was, she left not only her water pot but also her life. She ran into the city, saying, *"Come, see a man who told me all things that I ever did: is this not the Christ?"* It's not all about gathering within four walls, but being on the move for God.

For he said unto Abram, *"Get thee out of thy country, and from thy kindred, and from thy father's house, unto a land that I will shew thee."* That was the beginning of a new resolve, the result of being on the move for God. One said, *"I'll go if I must go alone."* But Jesus said, *"I am with you always, for I will never leave nor forsake you, even until the end of the world."* Remember the wilderness: a cloud by day, fire by night. Wherever he sends us, he is there. If more people are on the Lord's side, fewer shall be on the side of evil. Saul the persecutor became Paul the apostle, and by his hands God wrought special miracles. From his body were brought handkerchiefs and aprons, and disease departed, and evil spirits fled.

When my granddaughter had the coronavirus, she dwelt over fifty miles away, and I could not be there because it is contagious. But the Word of God was not hindered. He sent his Word, and she was healed. Each time I think about it, I must give him praise.

If faith, about the size of a mustard seed, can move a mountain, what then shall be wrought when God's people rise up together and get on the move for God?

Topic: "God's Timing is Always Right"

Genesis 16:1-5

¹Now Sarai Abram's wife bare him no children: and she had an handmaid, an Egyptian, whose name was Hagar. ²And Sarai said unto Abram, Behold now, the LORD hath restrained me from bearing: I pray thee, go in unto my maid; it may be that I may obtain children by her. And Abram hearkened to the voice of Sarai. ³And Sarai Abram's wife took Hagar her maid the Egyptian, after Abram had dwelt ten years in the land of Canaan, and gave her to her husband Abram to be his wife. ⁴And he went in unto Hagar, and she conceived: and when she saw that she had conceived, her mistress was despised in her eyes. ⁵And Sarai said unto Abram, My wrong be upon thee: I have given my maid into thy bosom; and when she saw that she had conceived, I was despised in her eyes: the LORD judge between me and thee.

Genesis 18:11-14

¹¹Now Abraham and Sarah were old and well stricken in age; and it ceased to be with Sarah after the manner of women. ¹²Therefore Sarah laughed within herself, saying, After I am waxed old shall I have pleasure, my lord being old also? ¹³And the LORD said unto Abraham, Wherefore did

Sarah laugh, saying, Shall I of a surety bear a child, which am old? [14]Is any thing too hard for the LORD? At the time appointed I will return unto thee, according to the time of life, and Sarah shall have a son.

Using for a subject, *"God's Timing Is Always Right,"* and the result is the greatest impact and fulfillment of his purpose. God doesn't always come before anything happens, but oftentimes he comes after to demonstrate his authority. No man will ever know that God can make all right until the need itself is present. God promised Abram, *"I will make thee a great nation,"* which implies offspring, and yet sometimes, before there can be addition, the need to take away must first take place. I could not do this on my own. This cannot be wrought by human skill; it must come by the power of God. Abram wanted to know what God would give him, seeing that he was childless. God told him, *"Out of thine own bowels shall thy seed be."* I don't know if Sarai got wind of this and, moving ahead of God, decided to put her own plan in notion. Yet God's will must be done in God's way. Just as the proverb says, "Thou canst not hurry God; thou must wait and give him time, or rather, wait on his time, for all time belongeth unto God."

Even Moses could not hasten God's deliverance of Israel into the promised land. After the spies returned and the people tempted the Lord, God commanded Moses, "Tomorrow turn you, and get you into the wilderness by the way of the Red Sea." That which was wrought apart from God proved fruitless; many died in the wilderness and had no second chance.

Scripture tells us that Sarai, Abram's wife, bare him no children and that she had a handmaid, an Egyptian named Hagar. Just as Adam allowed Eve to transgress the Word, so Abram took the words of Sarai and broke in upon the promise of God. Some boast, "I am the man of this house," yet here it seems the wives bore the ruling. We can't fix some things for ourselves and say that God did it, because he allowed it to happen, for that which starts with God must end with God. God's timing is always right.

Sarai said to Abram, "Behold, the Lord hath restrained me from bearing; go in unto my maid, that I may obtain children by her." Abram hearkened to the voice of Sarai. Yet God had plainly said that the heir should come of Abram's own bowels; had Sarai meant to share in the scheme, God would have told her so.

There is a saying, "*If I need thy help, I'll ask thee.*" Thus, Sarai took Hagar after Abram had dwelt ten years in the land of Canaan and gave her to Abram to be his wife. In those days, such a course was lawful when a wife could not conceive. But not in this case because it was interfering with God's plan. Hagar conceived. Perhaps Sarai thought her scheme had worked, yet as the song saith, "*Trouble in my way, I have to cry sometime.*" For, as the saying goes, she had opened a can of worms: not only was Hagar swollen with a child, but she was also swollen with pride. "*Look at me, Sarai,*" she seemed to boast, "*I have done what thou couldst not do.*" No longer bearing the spirit of a handmaid but lifted with a sense of superiority. Such was the fruit of Sarai's choice to take matters into her own hand.

David declared, "I waited patiently for the Lord, and he inclined unto me and heard me cry."

Job said, "If a man die, shall he live again? All the days of my appointed time will I wait, till my change come." Jeremiah said, "The Lord is good unto them that wait for him, to the soul that seeketh him." But Sarai put her foot in her mouth and blamed Abram for the plight, saying, "My wrong be upon thee; I gave my maid into thy bosom: and when she saw that she had conceived, I was despised in her eyes." Had she called upon the Lord, she might have found his help; he loveth those that seek him early. Abram may not have known what pride would rise in Hagar; such is the fruit of taking matters into one's own hands rather than waiting on the Lord. In time, God's plan came to pass. God' timing is always right.

Some changes first had to be made, as the song saith, "I know I've been changed; God done changed my name." My little grandson, Alex, once thought my daddy could do wondrous things because he made some ice cream from home. Ordinary men marvel at small things. When the norm is, if you want ice cream, you go to the store and buy it. Yet nothing is above God's expectations; he is supreme, and that which will do is impossible to man. Consider Genesis 18 and 19, when the messengers asked, "Where is thy wife?" Abraham answered, "Behold, in the tent."

Sarah's involvement was at hand, though she had earlier laughed within herself, "After I am waxed old, shall I have pleasure? And my Lord is old also?" Yet God can make the barren to bring forth; he raiseth up that which is dead to life.

Verse 10: *And he said, "I will certainly return unto thee according to the time of life, and Sarah thy wife shall have a son."* Having a child within the childbearing years is of the ordinary; but God is about to do the extraordinary. *Where wast thou, Job, when I laid the foundations of the earth? O Lord, our Lord, how excellent is thy name in all the earth, who hast set thy glory above the heavens? Hast thou, Job, an arm like God, or canst thou thunder with a voice like him?* God is about to take that which is barren and cause it to bring forth.

Now Abraham and Sarah were old and well stricken in age. *One day is with the Lord as a thousand years, and a thousand years as one day.* Perhaps you have heard it said, "Time is of the essence," but not so with God, for he is in control of time. And it had ceased to be with Sarah, after the manner of women, no longer in a childbearing state. Yet God can take that which is dead and bring it back into a state of life.

God told Abraham, "I will establish my covenant between me and thee, and thy seed after thee in their generations, for an everlasting covenant." Abraham had two sons: one by the bondmaid and the other by the free woman. He that was of the bondwoman was born after the flesh; he of the free woman was born by promise. Therefore, Sarah scoffed within herself, yet God's purpose reached beyond mere laughter; it looked to the setting up of a lineage to bring forth a Savior. God will raise up a prophet, yea, from the midst of Abraham's seed; generations shall hearken.

As Bartimaeus cried, "Thou Son of David, have mercy on me," so we cry for mercy. The Lord said, "Wherefore did Sarah laugh?" Grow in grace and in the knowledge of our Lord; receive his word, and take him at his word. Age has nothing to do with it, and we can ask ourselves if anything is too hard for the Lord. "Who are we that he should be hindered?" Nothing is too hard for the Lord. The Scriptures teach us not to think within ourselves, "We have Abraham as our father," for God is able out of these stones to raise up children unto Abraham. With God, nothing shall be impossible; his timing is ever right. A worldly song saith, "Nighttime is the right time to be with the one you love," yet every time is the right time to do that which is right. God looks beyond our faults and sees our needs, and his time is always right.

I testify of a time when sickness pressed me nigh unto death. It didn't come while I was still in Gadsden, but I was at the hospital; Mayday was called, and people came in with life-saving instruments. I remember tubes, and I remember when my heart ceased, and I entered a state as one without breath. I don't even know when Sharon was born that day, but I do know that two lives were saved that day. And I owe it all to the Lord.

In my days of service in hospitals, I saw people hooked to life-support machines. Some returned, some did not. Life and death are in the hands of the Lord. As 1 Samuel declares, "The Lord killed, and maketh alive; He bringeth down to the grave, and bringeth up." If you are steadfast in Jesus, death is but the gate to eternal life.

Thus, may I say, like Paul: to live is Christ, and to die is gain.

Topic: "A Return to the Image of God"

Genesis 1:26-28

[26]And God said, Let us make man in our image, after our likeness: and let them have dominion over the fish of the sea, and over the fowl of the air, and over the cattle, and over all the earth, and over every creeping thing that creepeth upon the earth. [27]So God created man in his own image, in the image of God created he him; male and female created he them. [28]And God blessed them, and God said unto them, Be fruitful, and multiply, and replenish the earth, and subdue it: and have dominion over the fish of the sea, and over the fowl of the air, and over every living thing that moveth upon the earth.

1 Corinthians 15:20-22

[20]But now is Christ risen from the dead, and become the firstfruits of them that slept. [21]For since by man came death, by man came also the resurrection of the dead. [22]For as in Adam all die, even so in Christ shall all be made alive.

Using for a subject, *"A Return to the Image of God."* One meaning of the word "image" is the character or reputation of a person or thing as generally received. Another is something that closely resembles another. And the word "subdue" means to have control over, to gain the upper hand, and to keep in check, and the result will be peaceful tranquility.

For the scripture lets us know that *the heaven, even the heavens, are the Lord's, but the earth hath he given to the children of men.* This shows us that everything God made, he made with. And when he created all else, he used the power of speech, and it came into focus. But when he made man, he used his hands. He left his habitation and formed man out of the dust of the ground and breathed into his nostrils the breath of life, and man became a living soul—that part which is in the image of God, the part that never dies but is eternal. God did this for the purpose of divine connection.

Therefore, when God said unto the man and the woman, *"Be fruitful, and multiply, and replenish the earth, and subdue it,"* they were still in the image of God. But they left their first estate—the position of life—and the result was the position of death. We may say that Adam was a trailblazer: he blazed the trail of forbidden territory, that which God had said not to do. And thus, it came down to the point that *all have sinned and come short of the glory of God.*

Therefore, when David said, *"Behold, I was shapen in iniquity, and in sin did my mother conceive me,"* it had nothing to do with illegitimacy but with sin passed down from the one to whom God had said, *"Behold, I have given you every herb bearing seed, which is upon the face of all the earth, and every tree in which is the fruit of a tree yielding seed: to you it shall be for meat."* This lets us know that God knoweth what is best for that which he hath made. When he saw that Adam needed a helpmate, he created the woman. And he knows the result of what is forbidden and the harm it will bring.

For you see, in Scripture, there is both cursing and blessing: *"Do this, and you will be blessed; but if you refrain, the result is a curse."* David said, "I will bless the Lord at all times, and his praise shall continually be upon my lips." That is a shield against all that is contrary. God didn't stop with what was best for man; he extended his care to the animal kingdom, to every beast of the earth, every fowl of the air, and everything that creepeth upon the earth wherein is life, saying, *"I have given every green herb for meat, and it was so."* This shows us the result: perfection. Everything was in perfect order. *"And God saw everything that he had made, and behold, it was incredibly good. And the evening and the morning were the sixth day."*

Everything was set in order as God would have it: an open line of communication with the Almighty and every physical need supplied. Who would not wish to remain in such a setup? As David said, *"I will bless the Lord at all times, and his praise shall continually be in my mouth."* These are not mere words of admiration but power to shun evil and cling to what is good.

Had Adam stayed in the image of God, doing only that which was good, what a different world this would be today. The world itself is a living testimony of the ways of man; for had man stayed within the knowledge of God, oh, what a difference today would make.

Some say that Satan approached Eve because she was the weaker vessel, but God is no respecter of persons. He gives everyone the ability to choose what is right and avoid what is evil. *If any of you lack wisdom, let him ask of God, who giveth to all men liberally.* Not only to the male but also to the female.

For the Scripture says: *"Trust in the Lord with all thine heart, and lean not unto thine own understanding. In all thy ways acknowledge him, and he shall direct thy paths."* Therefore, when Satan said unto the woman, *"Ye shall not surely die, for God doth know that in the day ye eat thereof your eyes shall be opened, and ye shall be as gods, knowing good and evil,"* how could that which was made by God be compared with God Himself? Satan promised greater insight, but it was a lie. The warning remains: if anyone comes with anything different from what God has said, it must be rejected.

For Scripture again declares, *"Trust in the Lord with all thine heart, and lean not unto thine own understanding. In all thy ways acknowledge Him, and He shall direct thy path."* Thus, we know that we cannot be gods, but we can be of God. *Whosoever shall exalt himself shall be abased, and he that humbleth himself shall be exalted.*

King David gives us a firm example. To be somebody in the sight of God, one must first become a nobody to himself. When he brought the ark of God to the city of David in the right way, it is said that he danced naked before the Lord. His nakedness was not the absence of clothes but the laying aside of kingly appearance. He came before God as an empty pitcher before a full fountain. He laid down his title as *King David* and humbled himself before the Lord. For God is in heaven, and we are upon the earth below; the only way to approach him is with humility.

And though we stand guilty before the world, all is not lost. We still have the chance to be restored to the image of God. There's a song of the world that says, "You are good even when you are bad." But only God is good, even when we are bad. Oh, how sweet it is to be loved by God! For the world is a living testimony of how many have sinned, yet it doesn't hinder the love of God.

The first Adam brought sin into the world, but the second Adam came to undo what the first had done, restoring fellowship with the Almighty. He talks to us, and we can talk to him. No longer can we say, "The devil made me do it," for *greater is he that is in me than he that is in the world.* That "he" is Jesus Christ.

Some say it is "in their blood," but we live no longer by our own blood. We have been washed by the blood of Jesus. Before God created, he knew sin would come to pass; therefore, he made preparation beforehand. *All things work together for good to them that love God, to them who are called according to his purpose.* And that purpose is to be conformed to the image of his Son. If he does not see Jesus in me, then no confession of lips will suffice. All of life must be under his ordination.

For Scripture warns, "*When the king came in to see the guests, he saw there a man who had not on a wedding garment.*" The garment is provided by Jesus. Without it, we shall not enter into his rest. When Jesus said, "*Whosoever eateth my flesh and drinketh my blood hath eternal life, and I will raise him up at the last day,*" he spoke not of the physical but of the spiritual. Without him dwelling within, there will be no resurrection into eternal life. He gave us this example himself: when the time came to return to the Father, he descended while the witnesses watched. And I long to be where Jesus is.

This calls us to return to, and remain in, the reflection of God. The first Adam brought sin, but the second Adam brought redemption. No longer bound by sin, but clinging to what is good, we are given another chance to be remade in the image of God. *For God, sending his own Son in the likeness of sinful flesh, and for sin, condemned sin in the flesh,* that we might live for the glory of God. No longer of dead works contrary to his will, but heirs with Christ, seated at the right hand of God. What manner of love is this that Jesus laid down his life for the sins of man!

It is a love that sustains us even when life sets before us hard roads. We can still say, "Who shall separate us from the love of Christ?" Letting us know there is no plan better than God's plan, no matter how good another may sound. For Jesus himself hath said, "Lo, I am with you always, even unto the end of the world." No one else can give such assurance. Therefore, let us abide under the shadow of his wings.

Subject: "Staying with God No Matter What"

Genesis 22:1-10

[1]And it came to pass after these things, that God did tempt Abraham, and said unto him, Abraham: and he said, behold, here I am. [2]And he said, take now thy son, thine only son Isaac, whom thou lovest, and get thee into the land of Moriah; and offer him there for a burnt offering upon one of the mountains which I will tell thee of. [3]And Abraham rose up early in the morning, and saddled his ass, and took two of his young men with him, and Isaac his son, and clave the wood for the burnt offering, and rose up and went unto the place of which God had told him. [4]Then on the third day Abraham lifted up his eyes and saw the place afar off. [5]And Abraham said unto his young men, abide ye there with the ass; and I and the lad will go yonder and worship, and come again to you. [6]And Abraham took the wood of the burnt offering and laid it upon Isaac his son; and he took the fire in his hand, and a knife; and they went both of them together. [7]And Isaac spake unto Abraham his father, and said, my father: and he said, Here am I, my son. And he said, Behold the fire and the wood: but where is the lamb for a burnt offering? [8]And Abraham said, my son, God will provide himself a lamb for a burnt offering; so they went both of them together. [9]And

they came to the place which God had told him of; and Abraham built an altar there, and laid the wood in order, and bound Isaac his son, and laid him on the altar upon the wood. [10]And Abraham stretched forth his hand and took the knife to slay his son.

Job 1:6-12

[6]Now there was a day when the sons of God came to present themselves before the LORD, and Satan came also among them. [7]And the LORD said unto Satan, Whence comest thou? Then Satan answered the LORD, and said, from going to and fro in the earth, and from walking up and down in it. [8]And the LORD said unto Satan, Hast thou considered my servant Job, that there is none like him in the earth, a perfect and an upright man, one that feareth God, and escheweth evil? [9]Then Satan answered the LORD, and said, Doth Job fear God for nought? [10]Hast not thou made an hedge about him, and about his house, and about all that he hath on every side? Thou hast blessed the work of his hands, and his substance is increased in the land. [11]But put forth thine hand now, and touch all that he hath, and he will curse thee to thy face. [12]And the LORD said unto Satan, Behold, all that he hath is in thy power; only upon himself put not forth thine hand. So, Satan went forth from the presence of the LORD.

Using for a subject *"Staying with God No Matter What."* No matter what the circumstances, whether they are favorable or not, the one that God said, *"Sarah thy wife shall bear thee a son indeed, and thou shalt call his name Isaac; and I will establish my covenant with him for an everlasting covenant, and with his seed after him."* But now God saith, *"Take now thy son, thine only son Isaac, whom thou lovest, and get thee into the land of Moriah; and offer him there for a burnt offering upon one of the mountains which I will tell thee of."* Abraham was being made ready to find out what he was made of. Just as it takes sunshine and rain to make a crop grow, it takes both advantages and disadvantages for a heart to stay in the right attitude with the Lord. Abraham didn't take his son and run to the hills, as some might do to escape their assignment from the Lord.

As Jonah did, but he found out there is no escape from God. Leaving town was of no avail. Abraham didn't need motivation from artificial intelligence in order to do as God said. And Isaac, his son, split the wood for the burnt offering, and they rose up and went unto the place which God had told him. The Scripture tells us that obedience is better than sacrifice, but in this case, it was both: Abraham being obedient to God in the sacrificing of his son. In other words, a winning combination was at work. As with Noah, *according to all that God commanded him, so did he.* As the scriptures tell us: be ye steadfast, unmovable, always abounding in the work of the Lord. The thing of God here was to offer Isaac for a burnt offering.

Then on the third day Abraham lifted up his eyes and saw the place afar off. I don't know what Abraham thought, but if it was me, I would have cried out, "Lord, help me to hold out!" The place to offer up my son was in sight. And Abraham said unto his young men, "*Abide ye here with the ass, and I and the lad will go yonder and worship, and come again unto you.*" If that's not faith, I don't know what faith is. For if he had killed his son, God would bring him back to life; that's why he said, "*I and the lad come again to you.*"

And Abraham took the wood for the burnt offering and laid it upon Isaac, his son, and he took the fire in his hand and a knife, and they went both of them together. Isaac, seeing he had everything needed except one, said unto his father, "Behold the fire and the wood, but where is the lamb for a burnt offering?" The reply was, "My son, God will provide himself a lamb." With the promises he had from the Lord concerning Isaac—and God does not lie—something miraculous was certain: if Isaac died, God would bring him back to life. That's why Abraham could tell the young men, "We will return."

And when he came to the place which God had told him of, Abraham built an altar there, and laid the wood in order, and bound Isaac, and laid him on the altar upon the wood. And Abraham stretched forth his hand and took the knife to slay his son, letting us know that nothing should be so precious in our lives that we hold it back from God. Abraham went to the fullest extent one can go to prove his faith in God. Faith moved the knife from the body of his son unto a ram in the thicket. For God tested Abraham to see where his fate lay, and we can say, as the saying goes, *he passed with flying colors*. You see, we need to know for our own benefit what we are made of, and everything that ought not to be must be stumped underfoot and cast into the brook Kidron, where idols are destroyed. *Staying with God no matter what.* For in that same location where Abraham offered up Isaac, Solomon built the temple, telling us that if we would be of the church of God, we must do as he saith, for it is the place where God can take that which is dead spiritually and bring it back to life.

As Paul said, "*When I am weak, then am I strong; less of me and more of God.*" Then the scriptures let us know, "*There was a man in the land of Uz, whose name was Job; and that man was perfect and upright, and one that feared God and eschewed evil.*" It gave in detail exactly who Job was. No fault was found in him, as Pilate said concerning Jesus, "*I find no fault in this man.*" Now there was a day when the sons of God came to present themselves before the Lord, and Satan came also among them, letting us know that Satan is a church-going Satan, seeking to take away from God those he does not yet have. The Lord said unto Satan, "*Whence comest thou?*" Then

Satan answered the Lord and said, "*From going to and fro in the earth, and from walking up and down in it.*" Not only Satan, but everybody must give an account before the Lord. For the scripture tells us, "*There was a certain rich man which had a steward; and the same was accused unto him that he had wasted his goods. And he called him and said, How is it that I hear this of thee? Give an account of thy stewardship, for thou mayest be no longer steward.*" You see, it is not just Satan, but us all.

And the Lord said unto Satan, "*Hast thou considered my servant Job?*" Sometimes, in my going through, I ask the Lord, "Did you give Satan permission to test me?" But I press on the upward way, gaining new heights every day. And everything that comes against me I can say, like Paul, "I count it as dung." And also, I can say, like David, "Yea, though I walk through the valley of the shadow of death, I will fear no evil, for thou art with me; thy rod and thy staff they comfort me." And again, I can say, like Paul, "To live is Christ, and to die is gain." Who wouldn't want that?

Then Satan answered the Lord and said, "*Doth Job fear God for naught?*" He was saying that if Job didn't have the blessings he had, he would not have the godliness he professed. *Take it away, and you will see what the real Job is about. Hast thou not made a hedge about him, and about his house, and about all that he hath on every side? Thou hast blessed the work of his hands, and his substance is increased in the land.* But these things were accounted to Job because of who he was beforehand, no matter his physical state. It was the result of a right relationship with God. And he did the right thing with what he had. Therefore, Satan told the Lord, "*Put forth thine hand now, and touch all that he hath, and he will curse thee to thy face.*" Satan was looking at Job's outward appearance, but God was looking at his heart. So God said, "*Behold, all that he hath is in thy power; only upon himself put not forth thine hand.*" So Satan went forth from the presence of the Lord.

And so the test began. But as David said, *"Shew thy marvellous loving kindness, O thou that savest by thy right hand them which put their trust in thee from those that rise up against them."* Satan was about to find out who Job really was, and not the Job he imagined. When Job thought it was God doing these things—the loss of his children, servants, and livestock—he arose, rent his mantle, shaved his head, fell down upon the ground, and worshipped. *Staying with God no matter what.* For he said, *"Naked came I out of my mother's womb, and naked shall I return thither. The Lord gave, and the Lord hath taken away; blessed be the name of the Lord."*

When Satan saw this didn't deter Job, he asked God to go further. You see, nothing can happen, good or bad, without God's consent. *Put forth thine hand now, and touch his bone and his flesh, and he will curse thee to thy face.* And when Satan had finished what he did, then came the voice, *"Curse God, and die."* But in all this, Job did not sin but held fast to his integrity. And the result was that his latter end was greater than his beginning. As James said, "Behold, we count them happy which endure. Ye have heard of the patience of Job, and have seen the end of the Lord: that the Lord is very pitiful, and of tender mercy." And "pitiful" here means "full of compassion," for he cares for the needs of his people.

For we need him more than food for the stomach. As Jesus said, *"Man shall not live by bread alone, but by every word that proceedeth out of the mouth of God."* For the word caused Job to triumph over his affliction. First, it gave him the ability to forbear. While asking the Lord what he would have me say, the times I was hospitalized with a blood clot in my leg came into my thoughts. If it had moved to my heart, my brain, or my lungs, the result would have been a stroke, heart attack, or even death. But those thoughts were not in my mind, for Jesus kept me in perfect calm. The first time I stayed in the hospital, I was twenty years old, and I wouldn't eat the food. The doctor told me, "If you don't eat, we will feed you intravenously." I didn't know what that meant until they came in with a bottle, a tube, and a needle. King Jesus is my intravenous medication. He modified the result of what could happen. He is a continuous flow into my heart. In this, I can avoid the evil and seek the good, which is required to obtain eternal life. And I don't need to put my hand into his wounded side to accept him for who he is.

When we were children, one of my brothers wrote a letter to a girl, and it read, "I was sitting at the table eating fish, and I thought about you, baby, and I ate the damn dish. When I think of the goodness of Jesus, as Job said, All the while my breath is in me, and the spirit of God is in my nostrils, my lips shall not speak wickedness, nor my tongue utter deceit." As Abraham went to the utmost for God, King Jesus went to the utmost for us all, so we can go to the utmost for him. For the scripture tells us, "*In all thy ways acknowledge him, and he shall direct thy paths.*" For that which is contrary does not always come from doing wrong, but from doing right and refusing to do the wrong. As David said, "The Lord is my light and my salvation; whom shall I fear? The Lord is the strength of my life; of whom shall I be afraid?" No longer of the darkness but of the light. *Staying with God no matter what.*

Paul is known as an apostle of Jesus Christ, a missionary, and an ambassador of Jesus Christ, yet he had a thorn in the flesh. For he said, "*For this thing I besought the Lord thrice, that it might depart from me. And he said unto me, My grace is sufficient for thee, for my strength is made perfect in weakness.*" Then Paul said, "*Most gladly therefore will I rather glory in my infirmities, that the power of Christ may rest upon me.*" Weak in the flesh but strong in the Lord, letting us know that disadvantages are not always an evil report but sometimes keep one closer to the Lord. For we sometimes say, "If I get too high, Lord, bring me down," but he will not allow it in the first place when we are in a relationship with him.

For he keeps us in the standard we should be in. The result is *staying with God no matter what.* For as Joshua said unto Israel, *"As for me and my house, we will serve the Lord."* That is to stay with the Lord no matter what, for meek and humble is the way.

Subject: "A Promise Kept"

Deuteronomy 18:15-19

[15]The LORD thy God will raise up unto thee a Prophet from the midst of thee, of thy brethren, like unto me; unto him ye shall hearken; [16]According to all that thou desiredst of the LORD thy God in Horeb in the day of the assembly, saying, let me not hear again the voice of the LORD my God, neither let me see this great fire any more, that I die not. [17]And the LORD said unto me, they have well spoken that which they have spoken. [18]I will raise them up a Prophet from among their brethren, like unto thee, and will put my words in his mouth; and he shall speak unto them all that I shall command him. [19]And it shall come to pass, that whosoever will not hearken unto my words which he shall speak in my name, I will require it of him.

John 3:16-20

[16]For God so loved the world, that he gave his only begotten Son, that whosoever believeth in him should not perish, but have everlasting life. [17]For God sent not his Son into the world to condemn the world; but that the world through him might be saved. [18]He that believeth on him is not condemned: but he that believeth not is condemned already, because he hath not believed in the name of the only begotten Son of God. [19]And this is the condemnation, that light is come into the

world, and men loved darkness rather than light, because their deeds were evil. [20]For every one that doeth evil hateth the light, neither cometh to the light, lest his deeds should be reproved.

Using for a subject, *"A Promise Kept."* Unto them concerning the feast of the Lord, which ye shall proclaim to be a holy gathering, these are my feasts. The purpose was to show honor to the Lord for what he had done in their lives, bringing them out of bondage and sealing them as his people. And when it comes to verse three, this is what man is not to do: six days shall work be done, but the seventh day is the Sabbath of rest. God knows the limits of man; they do not have endless strength to go on without rest. The day of rest is a holy convocation, a time to give thanks unto the Lord. As David said, *"I was glad when they said unto me, let us go into the house of the Lord; our feet shall stand within thy gates, O Jerusalem."* You see, the Sabbath is for the benefit of man and not God. For if God were to take a day off, the world would not stand as it does today, for all things move by the power of God. Our minds cannot grasp what it would mean if God ever ceased his work. I'm glad the scripture tells us, "I will lift up mine eyes unto the hills, from whence cometh my help. My help cometh from the Lord, who made heaven and earth. He will not allow your foot to slip; he that keepeth thee will not slumber. Behold, he that keepeth Israel shall neither slumber nor sleep. He is always active for the sake of mankind.

He was there at the pool of Bethesda, while the feast of the Jews was going on. They were doing what God commanded, and Jesus—the Son of God, God in the flesh—was doing what he came to do. For he said, "I must work the works of him that sent me while it is day." He gave no restriction of day, for the Sabbath is set aside for man's rest and for turning to

God with thanksgiving for his saving acts in our lives. And if it were not for Jesus, there would be no Sabbath. For he said, "The Son of man is Lord also of the Sabbath," showing us that he knew its true purpose. The Sabbath is not about man telling God what to do, but God instructing man.

At Jerusalem, by the sheep market, there was a pool called Bethesda with five porches. In those days, a great multitude of impotent folks lay there, unable to help themselves. As Paul said, "I can do all things through Christ which strengthens me."

There was a man in that condition for thirty-eight long years, unable to get into the pool when the water was stirred. The able-bodied hurried in first and wouldn't help him. But Jesus showed that the first shall be last, and the last first. When Jesus saw him lying there, knowing he had been in that state a long time, he saith unto him, *"Wilt thou be made whole?"* Scripture tells us that nothing is hidden from God's sight. Instead of saying, "Make me whole," he shifted the blame, saying, "I have no man to put me in the pool when the water is troubled." He did not know who spoke to him. Just as the woman at the well did not know when she said, "Sir, give me this water that I thirst not."

Yet Jesus said unto him, "Rise, take up thy bed, and walk." And immediately the man was made whole, and took up his bed and walked.

Isaiah said, *"Then the eyes of the blind shall be opened, the ears of the deaf unstopped, the lame man leap, and the tongue of the dumb sing."* There is no forbidden day for God's power. As the saying goes, where does the elephant sit? Anywhere he wants. God does whatever he wills, whenever he wills. That is why I will do what Jesus says. If he says jump, I ask not why but how high. For he said, *"I am the vine, ye are the branches; he that abideth in me and I in him brings forth much fruit, for without me ye can do nothing."* When you do this, it brings life, and life more abundantly.

And he did what Jesus said, and he was restored whole like the others. In the case of the man with dropsy, whose body was swollen with fluid, he didn't need a doctor or medicine. For Jesus touched him, healed him, and let him go. What a mighty God we serve! Angels bow before him, and heaven and earth adore him. And not only that, Lazarus had been dead four long days. His body has begun to decay, as Martha said, "By this time he stinketh." Jesus showed that even in the worst situation, he can bring us out. He said to the woman caught in the act of adultery, *"Go and sin no more."* Jesus said unto Lazarus, *"Come forth."* And the one who was dead came out alive.

Have any of you ever been in a situation where the only help available was in Jesus Christ? I have. Through all I have endured, I didn't know pain could paralyze me so deeply. I could hardly call my daughter, Sharon, at the other end of the house. I thought I would be found dead in my bed by morning. Yet I prayed to the Lord. I asked, "Are you taking little sister too? If so, I can't stop it."

And I fell asleep talking with the Lord. But when morning came, I was able to get out of bed, though still in pain. As scripture says, *"Weeping may endure for a night, but joy comes in the morning."* And my morning came; I am no longer in that pain. From death's shadow, I found myself "back in the saddle again," back in sweet communion with Jesus. Who wouldn't serve a God like that? Outside of him is eternal damnation, but in him is eternal life.

This comes by doing what he said. The blind would not have seen unless they obeyed Jesus. The lame would not have walked unless they obeyed Jesus. Salvation will never come to the heart unless we do what Jesus said, *"Come unto me, all ye that labor and are heavy laden, and I will give you rest."* You do not have to go through this alone, for he is here. *"Take my yoke upon you and learn of me, for I am meek and lowly in heart, and ye shall find rest unto your souls."* A yoke is a crossbar that hook together and when one is hooked to Jesus on what a difference life is like for my yoke is easy and my burden is light, that heavy load of life comes into none-existence. As the song says, "I got rid of my heavy load by doing what Jesus said." And he never asks us to do a thing without giving the strength to do it.

Enter ye in at the strait gate. If not, the gate leadeth to destruction. Being yoked to Jesus is a partnership, a shared purpose. He has his part; we have ours. It is not only about what he does for us, but also what we do for him. As he said, *"Let your light so shine before men, that they may see your good works, and glorify your father in heaven."*

When Samantha, at a very young age, spoke words beyond her years, someone said, "She talks big girl talk."

One day in a McDonald's parking lot, she saw a toy in the window and started saying, "I want that toy." Jimmy went running inside, came back with a Happy Meal with the toy, but forgot the straw. He ran back in, returned with it, and Samantha said, "I can count on you, Jimmy, and you can count on me." In this random life, it's not only, "I can count on you, Jesus," but also, "Jesus, you can count on me."

Jesus found Philip and said, *"Follow me."* Philip found Nathanael and said, "We have found him of whom Moses and the prophets wrote, Jesus of Nazareth, the son of Joseph. For everybody ought to know who Jesus is. When the woman at the well discovered who he was, she left her water pot and went into the city, saying, "Come, see a man who told me all I ever did." When the man healed at Bethesda found out who Jesus was, he told the Jews, "It was Jesus who made me whole."

For Jesus said, "The law and the prophets were until John. But now, in Jesus, God himself has come in the flesh. No longer sending Moses to Pharaoh saying, "Let my people go." No longer sending Isaiah to say, "Come, let us reason together." No longer sending Jonah to Nineveh to cry against its wickedness. For now Jesus says, *"Behold, I stand at the door and knock. If any man hears my voice and opens the door, I will come in and sup with him, and he with me."*

Topic: "God has a Purpose for Every Situation and a Situation for Every Purpose"

Esther 4:13-14

[13]Then Mordecai commanded to answer Esther, Think not with thyself that thou shalt escape in the king's house, more than all the Jews. [14]For if thou altogether holdest thy peace at this time, then shall there enlargement and deliverance arise to the Jews from another place; but thou and thy father's house shall be destroyed: and who knoweth whether thou art come to the kingdom for such a time as this?

Using the subject, *"God has a Purpose for Every Situation and a Situation for Every Purpose,"* the scripture lets us know that for everything there is a season and a time for every purpose under heaven. A time to be born, and a time to die; a time to plant, and a time to pluck up that which is planted; a time to kill, and a time to heal; a time to break down, and a time to build up; a time to weep, and a time to laugh; a time to mourn, and a time to dance; a time to cast away stones, and a time to gather stones together; a time to embrace, and a time to refrain from embracing; a time to get, and a time to lose; a time to keep, and a time to cast away; a time to sow, and a time to reap; a time to keep silence, and a time to speak; a time to love, and a time to hate; a time of war, and a time of peace.

Mordecai's words to Esther were: *"Who knows whether thou art come to the kingdom for such a time as this, put in this place for this purpose."* We can all say that God's timing is always right, not too early and not too late. He knows the right moment to bring the greatest impact. I have heard people use the term "milk it," allowing it to climb to its height so he can bring it to naught, to show man that nothing is too hard for the Lord. Therefore, he didn't resolve the situation while it was in its minor stage but allowed it to rise to the max, knowing he was going to bring it to naught.

For you see, time controls the activity of man, but God controls the activity of time. Nothing catches God by surprise; he knows the end before they even begin. The first eight verses of Ecclesiastes, the third chapter, tell how man is governed by time, but from Genesis to Revelation we see how time is governed by God, even before creation. He knew the ways of man before he made the first man and put him in the garden of Eden. He knew that Adam would sin before there was an Adam. For he let us know in his word, *"For whom he did foreknow, He also did predestinate to be conformed to the image of his Son, that he might be the firstborn among many brethren."* He knows the thereafter before they even come to pass.

In the Book of James, it is written, *"Go to now, ye that say, today or tomorrow we will go into such a city, and continue there a year, and buy and sell and get gain; whereas ye know not what shall be on the morrow. For what is your life? It is even a vapor that appeareth for a little time, and then vanisheth away. For that ye ought to say, if the Lord will, we shall live and do this or that."* This shows us that what is not in the will of God cannot happen by its own say-so; it is either his divine will or his allowed will, and each hath its purpose.

He allowed the descendants of Abraham for his divine purpose, for in order to be a people of God, deliverance must take place. And to show man that every purpose of the Lord shall stand, and all that is contrary will one day be done away with. For there is a test that one must pass: *He that saith, I know him, and keepeth not his commandments, is a liar, and the truth is not in him. But whoso keepeth his word, in him verily is the love of God perfected. Hereby know we that we are in him.*

In the miracle of the feeding of the five thousand, Jesus tested Philip, the same Philip who had said to Nathanael, "We have found him of whom Moses in the law and the prophets wrote, Jesus of Nazareth."

Moses had said, "The Lord thy God will raise up unto thee a Prophet; unto him ye shall hearken."

Isaiah declared, "And there shall grow out of his roots a branch."

Jeremiah said, "Behold, the days come, saith the Lord, that I will raise unto David a righteous Branch, and a King shall reign and prosper, and shall execute judgment and justice in the earth."

And Daniel said, "I saw in the night visions, and, behold, one like the Son of man came with the clouds of heaven, and came to the Ancient of days, and they brought him near before him. And there was given him dominion, and glory, and a kingdom, that all people, nations, and languages, should serve him. His dominion is an everlasting dominion, which shall not pass away, and his kingdom that shall not be destroyed."

The same Jesus turned to Philip and said, "Whence shall we buy bread, that these may eat?" Jesus already knew what he would do. He would take what was available, bless it, and make it more than enough. For he is that kind of God; he can take what little we have, no matter the amount, and bring forth sufficiency.

When God assessed Abraham, it was not in the natural but in the supernatural, for Abraham had the kind of faith that believes God can raise the dead. When God said to him, *"Take now thy son, thine only son Isaac, whom thou lovest, and get thee into the land of Moriah; and offer him there for a burnt offering upon one of the mountains which I will tell thee of,"* Abraham rose up early in the morning. He set himself to be where God wanted him to be, not saying, "I'll get there when I get there," but rising to obey. Before they went up to the mountain, he said to the young men, *"Abide ye here with the ass; I and the lad will go yonder and worship and come again to you."*

For you see, God had already said unto Abraham, *"Wherefore did Sarah laugh, saying, Shall I of a surety bear a child, which I am old? Is anything too hard for the Lord?"* You can trust him at his word.

When Joshua prayed, he said before Israel, "Sun, stand thou still upon Gibeon; and thou, Moon, in the valley of Ajalon." And the sun stood still, and the moon stayed until the people had avenged themselves upon their enemies.

When Hezekiah was sick unto death, after praying, God sent Isaiah to tell him that fifteen years would be added to his life. Yet Hezekiah asked for a sign. And the Lord caused the sundial of Ahaz to turn backward ten degrees, showing that time itself is under his control.

Abraham stretched forth his hand to slay his son, but the angel of the Lord interrupted him, "Lay not thine hand upon the lad." Abraham had proven himself faithful unto the Lord. Not your son, Abraham, but mine shall be offered up for the sins of the world. God's timing is always right.

Out of hatred for one man, a Jew, Haman plotted the destruction of all the Jews. But God's eyes are upon the ways of man, and he sees all his goings. *There is no darkness, nor shadow of death, where the workers of iniquity may hide themselves.* He overthrows the plans of the proud. He strikes down the wicked in the open sight of others because they turned their backs on him and would not consider his ways. Yet he hears the cry of the poor and the afflicted. *When he gives quietness, who then can make trouble? And when he hides his face, who then can behold him?*

Haman schemed that the Jews should be massacred. But just as God had provided a ram for Abraham, he had prepared a queen in the palace. When Esther became queen, God already had a ram in the bush. He did not stop Haman's plan at the beginning but let it rise to the point where he would bring it to nothing. For when man's plan collides with God's plan, we already know who prevails.

After receiving certification from the king, and sealed with the king's ring, letters were sent out by post to all of the king's provinces to destroy, to kill, and to cause to perish all Jews—both young and old, little children and women—at an appointed time of the year. I will not attempt here to recount every detail of what was taking place.

Haman thought Esther's banquet was to honor him, but he didn't know it was to expose him. He had an invitation for the purpose of his downfall. Nothing takes God by surprise, for he knows the end from the beginning. He allows adversity to rise so he can demonstrate his authority and remind man that he does not have the final word. What is meant for evil, God can turn to good, for his timing is always right.

When the appointed time came, the Jews fought for their lives, and with the help of God, they overcame their enemies. *If God be for us, who can be against us?* As the saying goes, "A winner cannot lose, and a loser cannot win," for God is an on-time God.

Some of man's time is spent in sleep, but *he that keepeth Israel shall neither slumber nor sleep.* As the scripture says, "As for God, his way is perfect; the word of the Lord is tried: he is a shield to all them that trust in him."

God had promised David, *"When thy days be fulfilled, and thou shalt sleep with thy fathers, I will set up thy seed after thee, which shall proceed out of thy bowels, and I will establish his kingdom. He shall build a house for my name, and I will establish the throne of his kingdom forever."* That seed is Jesus Christ, born of the Virgin Mary. For to become a child of God, a new birth must take place, one not of man's will but of God's spirit.

As Jesus said unto Nicodemus, *"That which is born of the flesh is flesh; and that which is born of the Spirit is spirit."* The old life is crucified with Christ, that sin might be destroyed, and we no longer serve it. *I am crucified with Christ: nevertheless I live; yet not I, but Christ liveth in me. And the life which I now live I live by the faith of the Son of God, who loved me, and gave himself for me.*

The ways that once seemed right, Paul said, I now count as loss. For to become a child of God is only by faith in Jesus Christ. And there is a day yet to come; we know not the day nor the hour when the son of man shall return. But we know this: God's timing is always right.

Job said, "If a man die, shall he live again? all the days of my appointed time will I wait, until my change comes." And the Lord blessed the latter end of Job more than his beginning.

For he is an on-time God, yes, he is.

David said, "When I said, My foot slippeth; thy mercy, O Lord, held me up." Peter walked on the water toward Jesus, and when he began to sink, Jesus reached out and caught him by the hand.

He is an on-time God, and I know it for myself. I could have been dead a long time ago, gone into cardiac arrest, been resuscitated, or been placed on life support, but that same day, strength returned to me. None but Jesus. Another chance to get in a right relationship with the Lord.

As Jesus said, "I and my father are one. Being one with God is the greatest strength. Who shall separate us from the love of Christ?" Nothing past, nothing present, and nothing to come can separate us from his love.

As the song says, "It is all right now, for I have given my heart to Jesus, and it is all right now. For greater is he that is in me than he that is in the world." He gives us strength to press toward the mark for the prize of the high calling of God in Christ Jesus.

From glory to glory, the old self is gone, and a new creation stands in Christ Jesus.

They say the president's visit to South Carolina State College in Orangeburg was a historic event, but the greatest event is to have one's name written in the Lamb's Book of Life. For then, man is no longer bound by time. There are no fewer days but life eternal.

Topic: "Staying in the Right Lane"

Hebrews 6:1-8

[1]Therefore leaving the principles of the doctrine of Christ, let us go on unto perfection; not laying again the foundation of repentance from dead works, and of faith toward God, [2]of the doctrine of baptisms, and of laying on of hands, and of resurrection of the dead, and of eternal judgment. [3]And this will we do, if God permit. [4]For it is impossible for those who were once enlightened, and have tasted of the heavenly gift, and were made partakers of the Holy Ghost, [5]and have tasted the good word of God, and the powers of the world to come, [6]if they shall fall away, to renew them again unto repentance; seeing they crucify to themselves the Son of God afresh, and put him to an open shame. [7]For the earth which drinketh in the rain that cometh oft upon it, and bringeth forth herbs meet for them by whom it is dressed, receiveth blessing from God: [8]but that which beareth thorns and briers is rejected and is nigh unto cursing; whose end is to be burned.

Galatians 2:11-14

[11]But when Peter came to Antioch, I withstood him to the face, because he was to be blamed. [12]For before that certain came from James, he did eat with the Gentiles: but when

they were come, he withdrew and separated himself, fearing them which were of the circumcision. [13]And the other Jews dissembled likewise with him; insomuch that Barnabas also was carried away with their dissimulation. [14]But when I saw that they walked not uprightly according to the truth of the gospel, I said unto Peter before them all, If thou, being a Jew, livest after the manner of Gentiles, and not as do the Jews, why compellest thou the Gentiles to live as do the Jews?

Using for a subject, *"Staying in the Right Lane."* A path or course that is prescribed for right living. One that does not turn to fit other circumstances. A path or route set for reasons of safety. The lane runner must stay in during a race. A starting point, and then moving on, and that is what these verses and the Hebrew scriptures are all about.

As Paul said, "When I was a child, I spoke as a child, I thought as a child; but when I became a man, I put away childish things." And even in putting away childish things, he also said, "Not as though I had already attained, or were already perfect; but I followed after…" What I do have is not all there is to achieve. That I may grasp that for which I was grasped by Jesus Christ. What I know is not all there is in Christ.

As the saying about artichoke hearts goes, you peel layer by layer until you reach the heart. There is something good at the heart. Perhaps you have heard someone say, "I have been to hell and back," but because of my knowledge of Jesus, it brought me back. And Paul also said, "I can do all things through Christ who strengthens me." The more I know, the more I grow in the grace of our Lord Jesus Christ, for it gives the strength to stand against the devil's schemes. Then we can say, like Jesus said, "Get thee hence, Satan." When spoken in the authority and power of Jesus, he has no choice but to leave.

The Hebrew scriptures tell us, *"Therefore leaving the principles of the doctrine of Christ, let us go on unto perfection; not laying again the foundation of repentance from dead works, and of faith toward God."* Just as the physical body needs a variety of foods for health, so spiritual health requires the whole Word of God. This keeps us from becoming spiritually stagnant. We must keep growing in the grace and knowledge of our Lord and Savior Jesus Christ.

This scripture teaches us that salvation was won for us by the crucified son of God and rests on the promise of God, who cannot lie. With this as our anchor, believers can look ahead with confidence and grow to maturity. No more crying, "Lord, save me," but standing firm: I am saved, sanctified, filled with the Holy Ghost, and on my way to heaven anyhow. That is the result of staying in the right lane, not only staying, but moving forward.

For there is more to know than just the doctrine of baptism, laying on of hands, the resurrection of the dead, and eternal judgment. Now that we have the milk of the Word, it is time to move on to the meat. When in school, one didn't stay in the stage of reading, writing, and arithmetic. Advancement had to be made. The same with the spiritual: the more you know, the more you grow, and this growth is seen in one's actions.

Verse 3 saith, *"And this we will do, if God permit,"* showing it is no longer of oneself, but that our marching orders are from the Lord. For *the steps of a righteous person are ordered by the Lord.* Every "go" must be a God-said-so, not what is contrary.

Therefore, let us consider the man of God from Judah and what happened to him when he went contrary to the Word of God. *For it is impossible for those who were enlightened and have tasted of the heavenly gift and were made partakers of the Holy Ghost and have tasted the good Word of God and the powers of the world to come…*All I can say is, I do not want to be one who turns back after tasting such things.

When I was sick, my complexion changed, but not my heart. For I know God will render to every man according to his deeds, to those who by patience in well-doing seek glory, honor, and immortality—eternal life. But to those who are contentious and do not obey the truth but follow unrighteousness, indignation and wrath, tribulation and anguish will come upon every soul that doeth evil, to the Jew first and also to the Gentile. But honor and peace to everyone who worketh good, to the Jew first and also to the Gentile. For there is no respect of persons with God.

Having tasted the good Word of God and the powers of the world to come, as the song saith, "I have decided to follow Jesus, no turning back." In the same way linen needs a stabilizer to hold its shape, Jesus is my stabilizer; He holds me steady in the right path.

Therefore, as the Hebrew scriptures says, "It is impossible if they shall fall away to renew them again to repentance, seeing they crucify to themselves the son of God afresh and put him to open shame. But the earth, which drinketh in the rain that falls upon it and bringeth forth herbs useful to those who farm it, receives blessing from God. As Psalm 65:10 saith, *"Thou waterest the ridges thereof abundantly; Thou settlest the furrows thereof; Thou makest it soft with showers; Thou blessest the springing thereof."*

But not like that which bears thorns and briers; it is rejected and near to cursing, whose end is to be burned. That is the result of being inducted into the army of the Lord but not keeping rank, being discharged by God. For it had been better not to have known the way of righteousness than, after knowing it, to turn from the holy commandment delivered. That is why I stay on the battlefield for my Lord, for this is not just about a dishonorable discharge but the loss of eternal life.

Staying in the right lane means staying in the things that accomplish salvation. A path or route set for safety, for *straight is the gate and narrow is the way, which leadeth unto life, and few there be that find it.*

There must also be elimination of the "wiggle room," getting rid of what is not necessary to remain in righteousness. Let us consider Peter. The Galatian scriptures tell us that when Peter came to Antioch, Paul withstood him to the face, because he was in the wrong. Peter began going the wrong way down a one-way lane.

Paul opposed him openly, for Peter had said out of his own mouth, "God hath shown me that I should not call any man common or unclean," when he was upon the housetop before being sent to Cornelius. And that word was meant for all men at all times. Yet before certain ones came from James, he ate with the Gentiles. But when they arrived, he withdrew and separated himself, fearing those of the circumcision. I knocked it down, for *the Lord is my shepherd; I shall not want.* Taking heed that man shall not live by bread alone, but by every word that comes from the mouth of the living God. For greater is he that is in me than he that is in the world.

But for those of the circumcision, I would remind them that it is no longer about the circumcision of the flesh but of the heart. As Paul said, "Follow me, as I follow Christ." Peter should have stayed with his Gentile brothers in Christ, instead of separating himself. For Christ came not only to unite God and man but also man and man. One nation under God, with liberty and justice for all.

The purpose of the Jewish nation was to live a godly life so that other nations would desire what they had. For in this, *"Thou shalt not covet"* does not apply. But the other Jews also followed Peter's example, so much so that Barnabas himself was carried away with them. This shows me to test the spirit by the Spirit to see whether it is of God. And when it is not of God, action must be taken.

For being in Christ is not just a me-myself-and-I thing but also one of others. Paul said, "When I saw they walked not uprightly according to the truth of the gospel, I said unto Peter before them all: If thou, being a Jew, livest after the manner of the Gentiles, and not as do the Jews, why compellest thou the Gentiles to live as the Jews?"

The best way to settle this is to live as Jesus lived, the perfect example of God's requirements. When we do as Jesus did, we are right at all times. And if I fall short, care enough for me to correct me. As Paul told Timothy, "Them that sin rebuke before all, that others also may fear," for none has advantage over another. We were all sheep going astray but are now returned unto the Shepherd and Bishop of our souls.

It was in the news about a golfer who made a hole-in-one from a very long distance. They thought that was something. But let us consider what Jesus did. He came into the world so that the world, through him, might be saved. Not living for oneself but becoming a new creation in Christ Jesus. The result: holy living.

Sermon Title: The Gift That Keeps on Giving

Luke 2:1-7

[1]And it came to pass in those days, that there went out a decree from Caesar Augustus, that all the world should be taxed. [2](And this taxing was first made when Cyrenius was governor of Syria.) [3]And all went to be taxed, everyone into his own city. [4]And Joseph also went up from Galilee, out of the city of Nazareth, into Judaea, unto the city of David, which is called Bethlehem; (because he was of the house and lineage of David): [5]To be taxed with Mary his espoused wife, being great with child. [6]And so it was, that, while they were there, the days were accomplished that she should be delivered. [7]And she brought forth her firstborn son, and wrapped him in swaddling clothes, and laid him in a manger; because there was no room for them in the inn.

Acts 2:37-41

[37]Now when they heard this, they pricked in their heart, and said unto Peter and to the rest of the apostles, men and brethren, what shall we do? [38]Then Peter said unto them, repent, and be baptized every one of you in the name of Jesus Christ for the remission of sins and ye shall receive the gift of the Holy Ghost. [39]For the promise is unto you, and to

your children, and to all that are afar off even as many as the Lord our God shall call. [40]And with many other words did he testify and exhort, saying save yourselves from this untoward generation, [41]then they that gladly received His word were baptized: And the same day there were added unto them about three thousand souls.

Using for a subject: *"The Gift That Keeps on Giving."* This gift can be shared with others, and the one who shares it still keeps it all! When a man gives a gift, he no longer has it. But when God gives a gift, there is no lack. Man's gift often bears the giver's name, but God's gift is for whosoever will. Man's gift is soon used up, but the gift God gives is eternal. Not the lights in the streets, but the light in the heart. For you see, when celebrating a person's birthday, it involves the one being celebrated. And as the saying goes, "Jesus is the reason for the season."

St. Matthew tells us that an angel of the Lord appeared unto Joseph, saying, "Thou son of David, fear not to take unto thee Mary thy wife, for that which is conceived in her is of the Holy Ghost." The Word that was with God, and was God, was planted in the womb of a virgin named Mary. In all other cases, except Adam and Eve, it took male and female to produce a child, and life began at birth. But Jesus existed before his birth, in the form of the Word. For scripture says, *"The Word was made flesh and dwelt among us, and we beheld His glory, the glory as of the only begotten of the Father, full grace and truth."*

The gift that keeps on giving. St. Luke tells us, "It came to pass in those days, that there went out a decree from Caesar Augustus, that all the world should be taxed." To everything there is a season, and a time to every purpose under heaven. God's plan was set in motion at the right time and at the right place. The taxing was made when Cyrenius was governor of

Syria, and all went to be taxed, each into his own city. Joseph went from Galilee, out of Nazareth, into Judea, unto the city of David, which is called Bethlehem, because he was of the house and lineage of David.

God used the stage set by man. Man's purpose was to count the people for taxation, but God's purpose was to show that people everywhere belong to Him. Obeying the decree, Joseph and his espoused wife Mary—near the end of her time—made the journey. With no room in the inn, they were placed in a stable. And that is where *Silent Night, Holy Night* began. Never a night like it before, and never again.

God knew the census took place. Later, in His adult life, Jesus said, "Render therefore unto Caesar the things that are Caesar's, and unto God the things that are God's," that is, our hearts. And as the song says, "Go tell it on the mountain, over the hills and everywhere, that Jesus Christ is born!"

Holy God became fashioned as man, the only one with two histories: God and man. The Holy Spirit joined deity and humanity in one person for the purpose of shaping Christ into our own character: The Gift That Keeps on Giving. A gift that can be shared with others, yet never runs out. I can understand the man Jesus healed, who was told not to tell anyone but went out and spread it widely. For when you've been touched by Jesus, you have to tell somebody! As the song says, "I can't keep it to myself!"

When I get my social security check, and when this one or that one gets theirs, once it is shared, there's little to none left. But I can share Jesus with the whole wide world and still have Him all!

The book of Acts tells us that when the people heard this, they were moved in their hearts and said to Peter and the rest of the apostles, "Men and brethren, what shall we do?" Letting you know, that same question—what shall we do—is still at hand. And the answer remains the same: repent and be baptized in the name of Jesus Christ for the forgiveness of sins. Without repentance and turning away, there is no real celebration of his birth, because his birth brings a new birth in us. And some took heed, for unto them were added about three thousand souls. Membership without Christ is no membership at all, for it must be about a new way of life.

Christmas is not about the lights that plug into a socket but about the light that shines in the heart, lit by Jesus Christ. For he is the light of the world, and without him, all is darkness. He is the gift that keeps on giving, not just for a chosen few, but for whosoever will. He is not a gift you keep to yourself but one you can share with all. Remember Paul and Silas, locked in jail with their feet in shackles. At midnight they prayed and sang praises to God, and the prisoners heard them.

Suddenly, there was a great earthquake; the foundations of the prison were shaken, the doors opened, and everyone's chains were loosed. Not for the sake of escape, but for a chance that somebody might know Jesus. Even the keeper of the prison cried out, *"What must I do to be saved?"* and not only he, but his whole household believed. That lets us know there is still a chance with Jesus.

The scripture also tells us about the child Samuel, who heard a voice calling him three times. Thinking it was Eli, he went to him. But Eli told him, "If you hear the voice again, say, 'Speak, Lord, for your servant is listening.'"

What a testimony it would be, on the day of celebrating Jesus's birth, for someone to receive a new birth of their own, to be born from above. For when the joy of Christmas fades away, the joy of Jesus will remain. When the Jews in Acts asked Him, *"Are you greater than our father Abraham?"* Jesus answered, *"Before Abraham was, I am."* He also said, *"Before the day was, I am He, and there is no other who can deliver out of My hand. I will work, and who shall stop it?"* Abraham may have been the head of the Jewish people, but Jesus is the head of eternal life. He is greater than the temple at the center of worship. Church membership without Jesus at the center is of no value.

Jesus is greater than Solomon, with all his wisdom and wealth, for if you turn from God, those things mean nothing. Greater than Jonah, who resisted God's blessing on the Gentiles. For Christ came not to call the righteous, but sinners to repentance. Greater than Jacob, who gave his people a well, for Jesus provided rivers of living water. Man was born innocent and became a sinner; Jesus was born holy and remained holy. Adam was the head of the human race, but Jesus is the head of the spiritual race. One came from the dust, the other the Spirit that will never die.

God blessed man with different talents to meet one another's needs. When you need good singing, you can call on Sister Teresa or Sister Sandra. When you need help with taxes, you can call on Brother Zeb. When your lawn mower breaks, you can call on Brother Sumpter. If you need a deck built, you can call on Brother Timothy. But for the saving of the soul, you must call on Jesus! People like to link themselves to many things to feel important, but the best link of all is with Jesus Christ. Some in the church at Corinth said, *"I am of Paul,"* or *"I am of Apollos,"* but the best is to say, *"I am of Christ,"* for by no other name can anyone enter eternal rest.

I can understand why the songwriter wrote, "Joy to the World, the Lord is Come." For what He came to do brings joy. Just as the birth of a child brings joy to the parents, the birth of Jesus brings joy to the whole world. For when we accept Him, what was in disarray is brought into order, what was broken is made whole. He told the man with the withered hand, *"Stretch forth thine hand."* And when he stretched it out, it was restored. The true celebration of Christmas is in the lives of those who have stretched themselves toward him, letting His birth live inside them. No longer the old self, but a new creation.

Then we can sing with a true heart, "Joy to the World, the Lord has come! Let earth receive her king!" I have received my king. My grandson, Alex, was very smart in school, and upon graduation, he received a lifetime scholarship. My goal is to achieve a lifetime citizenship in the Kingdom of God!

Topic: "Staying Where the Lord Puts One, Staying on the Right Road"

Genesis 12:10-13

[10]And there was a famine in the land: and Abram went down into Egypt to sojourn there; for the famine was grievous in the land. [11]And it came to pass, when he was come near to enter into Egypt, that he said unto Sarai his wife, behold now, I know that thou art a fair woman to look upon: [12]therefore it shall come to pass, when the Egyptians shall see thee, that they shall say, this is his wife: and they will kill me, but they will save thee alive. [13]Say, I pray thee, thou art my sister: that it may be well with me for thy sake; and my soul shall live because of thee.

Ruth 1:1-7

[1]Now it came to pass in the days when the judges ruled, that there was a famine in the land. And a certain man of Bethlehemjudah went to sojourn in the country of Moab, he and his wife, and his two sons. [2]And the name of the man was Elimelech, and the name of his wife Naomi, and the name of his two sons Mahlon and Chilion, Ephrathites of Beth-lehem-judah. And they came into the country of Moab and

continued there. ³And Elimelech Naomi's husband died; and she was left, and her two sons. ⁴And they took them wives of the women of Moab; the name of the one was Orpah, and the name of the other Ruth: and they dwelled there about ten years. ⁵And Mahlon and Chilion died also both of them; and the woman was left of her two sons and her husband. ⁶Then she arose with her daughters in law, that she might return from the country of Moab: for she had heard in the country of Moab how that the LORD had visited his people in giving them bread. ⁷Wherefore she went forth out of the place where she was, and her two daughters in law with her; and they went on the way to return unto the land of Judah.

Using for a subject: *"Staying Where the Lord Puts One, Staying on the Right Road."* And the result of making a wrong move. Again, I say, as the Word of God declares, man does not live by bread alone but by every word that proceeds from the mouth of God. If any changes are to be made, they will come from the Lord Himself.

Consider the circumstances of Abram. God told him, *"Get thee out of thy country, from thy kindred, and from thy father's house, unto a land that I will show thee."* Scripture tells us Abram's journey continued southward, teaching us to stand perfect and complete in all the will of God. But there was a famine in the land. Life consists not only food for the mouth but of God in the heart.

God sent an angel to say to Elijah, *"Arise and eat, for the journey is too great for thee."* And Elijah arose, ate, and drank, and went on the strength of that food forty days and forty nights, until he reached the place God wanted him to be. That same God had already spoken to Abram, saying, *"I am the Lord, I change not."* What he did for one, he would do for another. Yet because there was famine, Abram went down into Egypt, uncharted territory, unapproved by God.

The result of a wrong move is a change in thought, leading one into things they should never be involved in. In Egypt, Abram went seeking and gathering what was contrary to God's promise. He said to his wife Sarai, *"Behold, I know thou art a fair woman to look upon. When the Egyptians see you, they will say, 'This is his wife,' and they will kill me."* This was the same man God had promised to make a great nation, to bless, and to make his name great. A dead man cannot reproduce. Abram put fear of man before the word of God.

There is a saying: if you hunt for trouble long enough, you'll surely find it. Scripture shows us Abram found it. Instead of standing on God's word, he relied on his own theory, and it would have taken place if the Lord had not intervened. There's another saying, "Don't let your mouth write a check your body cannot cash." Don't speak what you cannot stand by later, for the cost may be more than you can repay. This reminds us not to get involved in anything that makes it appear God is less than who He says He is.

For when the devil said unto Jesus, "

If thou be the Son of God, cast thyself down, for it is written, He shall give His angels charge concerning thee, and in their hands they shall bear thee up," Jesus answered, *"It is written again, thou shalt not tempt the Lord thy God."* God had also said to Abram, *"Unto thy seed will I give this land."* Again—offspring from his body. And a dead man cannot reproduce. Yet Abram said to Sarai, *"Say, I pray thee, thou art my sister, that it may be well with me for thy sake, and my soul shall live because of thee"*

Abraham had put himself in a position where he couldn't say with David, *"Yea, though I walk through the valley of the shadow of death, I will fear no evil, for thou art with me; thy rod and thy staff, they comfort me."* The result of leaving the place God put him was fear and compromise. Scripture declares that Sarah was Abraham's wife. To deny any part of Scripture is to deny God Himself. Living by every word that proceeds from God means half-truth has no place in His plan. Yet God looked beyond Abram's flaws and saw his need. As the father restored the prodigal son with full honor, so Abram was restored his privileges.

There is enough in doing the will of God to occupy a whole lifetime. No room should be left for the contrary. Look at the result when people move from where God placed them. In the time of the judges there was famine, and another man made the wrong move. Instead of turning back to God, he sojourned in Moab, among the very people God had forbidden to enter His congregation. Scripture says, even to the tenth generation they shall not enter, for they met not Israel with bread and water and hired Balaam to curse thee.

How low can you go? By going to Moab, they were questioning the character of God—as if He was not who He said He was. Yet God had said to Abraham at ninety years old, *"I am the Almighty God. Walk before me, and be thou perfect."* God never asks without giving the ability to obey. He said to Moses, *"I am that I am. Tell the children of Israel, I am has sent me."* But still, a certain man of Bethlehem-Judah left where God had put him and went to sojourn in Moab. He, his wife, and two sons left the place of God's dwelling for a place where God dwelt not.

The result was a disaster. The men of the family died, leaving the woman alone. Choosing another path apart from God is dangerous. Naomi was left with her two sons and husband buried in foreign soil. Again, I say, as Scripture declares, *"Man shall not live by bread alone but by every word from the mouth of God."* The steps of God's people must be ordered by him alone.

When Israel stood before the Red Sea, with Pharaoh's army behind, Moses said, *"Stand still and see the salvation of the Lord."* His banner over us is love. They had left for food, but Naomi was left without life. There's a saying, "You better be on your P's and Q's when it comes to the things of God, for a time may come when it is too late.

Naomi later arose with her daughters-in-law to return, for she heard that the Lord had visited His people and given them bread. Not staying where the Lord puts us is the same as abandoning His word. God said to Abraham, *"To thy seed will I give this land."* They should not have departed but stayed. Wait on the Lord, be of good courage, and he will strengthen your heart.

And when rejoicing in the hope of the glory of God, hungry pains will pass. Letting us know also that it takes more than food for the stomach to survive. For when Naomi came back, they were still there. For God had kept them alive. For as the saying goes, "He is bread in a starving land, water in dry places, and by his hand I stand.

When I was a child, we were sharecropping, living on another's man's land, in a raggedy house.

We did all the labor; he got the increase. We were often hungry. One day while picking cotton, we came to the end of the row and found peas in the woods, ready to pick. He is an on-time God. Yes, He is. He may not come when you want Him, but He is always on time.

So I say, stay on the right road, for at the end stands the Lord. David said, "Wait on the Lord; be of good courage, and he shall strengthen thine heart. Wait, I say, on the Lord."

Job said, "If a man dies, shall he live again? All the days of my appointed time I will wait until my change comes."

Even if I lose a few things along the way—even brain cells, as I once joked with my pastor—I must remember who my Jesus is. He is the rock, my fortress, my deliverer, my strength, my buckler, my salvation, my high tower. And if I remember Him, that is enough.

Jesus came not with ease but with suffering. He said, *"I gave my back to the smiters, my cheeks to those who plucked my hair. I hid not my face from shame and spitting. The Lord God will help me, therefore I set my face like a flint."* This gave Paul courage to say, *"I am not ashamed of the gospel of Christ, for it is the power of God unto salvation."* It caused Nicodemus to seek Him by night. It caused the woman at the well to say, *"Come see a man."* It caused a leper to return with thanks, a woman with an issue to touch His garment, Zacchaeus to climb a tree.

At the close of His earthly work, He told His disciples, *"Yet a little while, and the world sees me no more; but ye see me. Because I live, ye shall live also."*

Don't settle for eye connections; seek heart reflections. As the song says, "I've got a telephone in my bosom, and I can call him up from my heart." Every day is not like Sunday, but He promised, "I will never leave thee nor forsake thee."

He stayed true to His mission, even on the road to Jerusalem where prophets had been killed, knowing He would be killed too. He came saying, *"A body thou hast prepared for me. I come to do thy will, O God."* Not with the blood of bulls and goats, but with His own blood.

On His way, He heard two blind men cry out, "Son of David, have mercy on us!" And He stopped to heal them. That same opportunity is still available today. The world may sing, "A little too late," but with Jesus, as long as there is breath, it is never too late. He is married to the backslider. His blood never loses its power.

And while I write this message, the word "intoxication" comes to mind, letting me know I can be intoxicated with Jesus and still walk straight, staying on the right road until the close of the day.

Topic: "Turning to a State of Reversal"

1 Kings 9:1-8

¹And it came to pass, when Solomon had finished the building of the house of the LORD, and the king's house, and all Solomon's desire which he was pleased to do, ²that the LORD appeared to Solomon the second time, as he had appeared unto him at Gibeon. ³And the LORD said unto him, I have heard thy prayer and thy supplication, that thou hast made before me: I have hallowed this house, which thou hast built, to put my name there for ever; and mine eyes and mine heart shall be there perpetually. ⁴And if thou wilt walk before me, as David thy father walked, in integrity of heart, and in uprightness, to do according to all that I have commanded thee, and wilt keep my statutes and my judgments: ⁵then I will establish the throne of thy kingdom upon Israel for ever, as I promised to David thy father, saying, There shall not fail thee a man upon the throne of Israel. ⁶But if ye shall at all turn from following me, ye or your children, and will not keep my commandments and my statutes which I have set before you, but go and serve other gods, and worship them: ⁷then will I cut off Israel out of the land which I have given them; and this house, which I have hallowed for my name, will I cast out of my sight; and Israel shall be a proverb and a

byword among all people: [8]and at this house, which is high, every one that passeth by it shall be astonished, and shall hiss; and they shall say, Why hath the LORD done thus unto this land, and to this house?

Using it for a subject, *"Turning to a State of Reversal."* The way it should be is not that way anymore. Reversal means to turn the other way, which is contrary. To change to the opposite character, moving in a direction outside the will of God, from the best to the worst. Not being careful about what is allowed in the house of God and what is allowed in one's own life. One might say, walking on unlevel ground where a fall is possible. For the scripture tells us, "What therefore God has joined together, let no man put asunder." It is not just about a marriage between a man and a woman but about his word to live by, which consists of do's and don'ts, and the results of them both.

Therefore, let us go on an expedition, exploring what God says man should do and what he should not. For he also said, "So shall my word be that goes forth out of my mouth; it shall not return void but shall accomplish what I please and prosper where I send it."

Starting in the garden of Eden, the Lord commanded the man, saying, "Of every tree of the garden thou mayest freely eat, but of the tree of knowledge of good and evil thou shalt not eat, for in the day thou eatest thereof thou shalt surely die." Where is Adam now? Dead.

And Abram, the one God told to get thee out of thy country, from thy kindred, and from thy father's house, unto a land I will show thee. The one God promised to make a great nation. Yet, because of a famine in the land, he went down into Egypt, allowing fear into his mind that he would be killed if it was known Sarah was his wife. But when you stay in the will of God, He has your back and your front.

As David said, yea, though I walk through the valley of the shadow of death, I will fear no evil, for thou art with me, thy rod and thy staff they comfort me.

For when one stays steadfast in the Lord, he lets us know when thou passest through the waters, I will be with thee; and through the rivers, they shall not overflow thee. When thou walkest through the fire, thou shalt not be burned, neither shall the flame kindle upon thee. No scars shall be left. It will be as though it never happened.

It is said Abraham lied when he called Sarah his sister. He didn't tell the whole truth, out of fear for his life. But the greater fault was that he didn't trust God. For the scripture says, The Lord shall preserve thy going out and thy coming in from this time forth, and even forevermore.

How many know that the sin of one can affect many? Therefore, the children of Israel could not stand before their enemies but turned their backs and fled, because of sin in the camp. God said, neither will I be with you anymore except ye destroy the accursed thing from among you. It was the doing of one man that caused such disarray. When Joshua confronted him, he confessed, I have sinned against the Lord God of Israel. And because of this, everything he stole, all that he possessed, was destroyed along with himself.

For the scripture tells us, but I say unto you, resist not evil; but whosoever shall smite thee on thy right cheek, action must take place. You can't allow what God disallows.

I heard one give a testimony about their lifestyle before they accepted Jesus Christ as Lord and Savior. And when they did, they said to their old ways: "You got to go, Buster." One cannot keep Buster and have Jesus Christ at the same time. For Jesus said, verily, verily, I say unto you, he that enters not by the door into the sheepfold but climbs up some other way, the same is a thief and a robber.

The difference is clear between what is welcome in and what must be sent away. We are not going to open our doors without a discernment of who enters. A sinner who comes into the house for repentance, the door stands on welcome hinges. Any other reason is like putting a bandage over an infected wound. It must be cleaned before healing can begin.

Again, the scripture tells us that some men's sins are open beforehand, going before judgment, and some follow after, showing up later. Not just putting wrong people in positions by giving out undeserved recognition or advancing what should be rebuked. It is necessary to hear from God before accepting the word of man.

For it came to pass that King David sat in his house, for the Lord had given him rest all around from his enemies. David said to Nathan the prophet, See now, I dwell in a house of cedar, but the ark of the Lord dwells within curtains. And Nathan said to the king, Go, do all that is in your heart, for the Lord is with you.

But just because he thought this thing, doesn't mean to do this thing. For God said, "*My thoughts are not your thoughts, neither are your ways my ways, saith the Lord. For as the heavens are higher than the earth, so are my ways higher than your ways, and my thoughts higher than your thoughts.*"

Therefore God sent Nathan back to David to tell him, *Thus saith the Lord, shalt thou build a house for me to dwell in?* letting him know he was not the one to build the house of the Lord. That was the end result. You see, obedience is better than sacrifice.

Hananiah was a false prophet, saying things God never sent him to say. There is a song that goes, You better mind, my brother, how you walk on this cross. If your right foot slips, your soul will be lost. God sent Jeremiah to tell Hananiah, I will cast thee from the face of the earth; this year thou shalt die. You see, it is a dangerous thing to fall into the hands of an angry God.

Not only did God let Solomon know the benefits of keeping his commandments and statutes but also the consequences if he turned away—a state of reversal. Again the scripture saith, Delight thyself also in the Lord, for the result is joy, fulfillment,, and no room for that which is contrary.

After the work of building the house of the Lord and the king's house was finished, we see it is all right to retire from physical labor, but there is no retirement from a relationship with Almighty God. As the saying goes, I'll go on and on if I have to go all by myself. For what we have obtained, there is still more to reach for. As Paul said, I press toward the mark for the prize of the high calling of God in Christ Jesus.

As the physical body needs daily bread to stay alive, so does the soul need a daily walk with the Lord to remain in His will. Therefore God appeared unto Solomon a second time and said, *"I have done what you asked of me, but there are stipulations that must be followed."* For you see, God is an "I will" God: *I will, if thou wilt walk before me as David thy father walked with integrity of heart, in uprightness, and according to all I have commanded thee.*

God does not ask one to do without giving the ability to do it. *"And I will keep my statutes,"* he says, letting us know this is conditional, that the heart must match the asking, and judgment must be in order for the thing to take place. Then God promised to establish the throne of Solomon's kingdom upon Israel forever. What amazing grace, an offer that should not be refused.

I have heard people say, You can take it to the bank, or put it in your pipe and smoke it. But when God makes a promise, you can take it to heart and seal it by remaining in His will. For He said, There shall not fail thee a man upon the throne of Israel; one from the line of David will always be king of his people. Thank God for Jesus, our everlasting King.

But verses 6 and 7 bring a warning: If you or your children turn away from following me and will not keep my commandments and statutes, which I have set before you, but go and serve other gods and worship them…God's word does not change from one generation to another. What He said to Solomon is not yesterday's word; it still stands today. Then will I cut off Israel from the land I have given them.

"One saved is always saved," not if one turns contrary to the will of God. And this house which I have hallowed for my name—I have left the building. Be careful what is allowed in the house of God. For He said, I will cast you out of my sight, and Israel shall be a proverb and a byword among all people.

It is a shame when those meant to be an example are instead looked upon with pity, or held up as a warning rather than a model of godliness. How low can one go? For it is better not to know the Lord than to know Him and turn away. For it had been better for them not to have known the way of righteousness, than, after they have known it, to turn from the holy commandment delivered unto them (2 Peter 2:21).

We say to Satan today: You are not part of this. Your profession without possession doesn't belong here. For in this house of God, which is high, no one will pass by astonished or hiss, saying, Why has the Lord done this unto this house? For this house is built upon the solid rock—not stones of earth, but the foundation of Jesus Christ.

For the scripture tells us, *Be ye steadfast, unmovable, always abounding in the work of the Lord.* And it also tells us: *Resist the devil and he will flee from you.* Do not take part in his schemes. The word says: *Put on the whole armor of God, that you may be able to stand against the wiles of the devil.* For everything we need to live a God-ordained life is written in his word.

We need no other addition to conclude the whole matter, for His word is not written in code, hidden from some and revealed to others. Everyone has a chance to know who Jesus is. The word gives warning: If any man shall take away from the words of this prophecy, God shall take away his part out of the book of life.

And again: Knowing this first, that no prophecy of the scripture is of any private interpretation. For prophecy came not in old time by the will of man, but holy men of God spoke as they were moved by the Holy Ghost.

God gave Solomon everything that he needed to live an obedient life, not by words from a prophet, but from the mouth of God Himself. Yet instead of staying in the will of God, he turned aside. As the Preacher, son of David, king in Jerusalem, said: *"Vanity of vanities, all is vanity."* Speaking of what it is like to no longer walk with God, the purpose of life unravels.

There is a saying: you don't miss your water till the well runs dry. Solomon missed the God-ordained life he once had with the Lord. Other things in life can be substituted one for another, but there is no substitute for God, not even procrastination, which is only a temporary display of what is not there. Pretending will come to the surface.

Let us not forget the one who pretended to be a scholar in Bible study, yet the outcome was far from it. This shows us the closeness of God is always necessary to guard against evil. Do not depend on hindsight, but on foresight. God gave Solomon foresight of what would happen if he failed to keep His commandments and statutes.

This lets us know that man does not live by bread alone, but by every word that proceeds from the mouth of God. I don't need a professor's degree to understand this, just a heart in tune with God. For scripture warns: *Beware lest any man spoil you through philosophy and vain deceit, after the traditions of men, after the rudiments of the world, and not after Christ. For in Him dwells all the fullness of the Godhead bodily.*

There was a song we sang as children: B-I-B-L-E, yes, that's the book for me. It stands alone, the word of God, the Bible—the book for me. Someone might take from me the material things, but they cannot take away what belongs to God. For who can separate us from the love of God which is in Christ Jesus?

And like the man Jesus healed, who was told not to tell anybody yet went about spreading it much, some things in life may be kept secret, but the word of God is not one of them, neither are his benefits.

Topic: "The Whole Counsel of God Must be Represented"

Psalm 49: 1-2

¹Hear this, all ye people; give ear, all ye inhabitants of the world: ²Both low and high, rich and poor, together.

Matthew 13:1-9

¹The same day went Jesus out of the house and sat by the sea side. ²And great multitudes were gathered together unto him, so that he went into a ship, and sat; and the whole multitude stood on the shore. ³And he spake many things unto them in parables, saying, behold, a sower went forth to sow; ⁴And when he sowed, some seeds fell by the way side, and the fowls came and devoured them up; ⁵some fell upon stony places, where they had not much earth: and forthwith they sprung up, because they had no deepness of earth. ⁶And when the sun was up, they were scorched; and because they had not root, they withered away. ⁷And some fell among thorns; and the thorns sprung up, and choked them, ⁸but other fell into good ground, and brough forth fruit, some an hundredfold, some sixtyfold, some thirtyfold, ⁹who hath ears to hear, let him hear.

Matthew 4:4

But he answered and said, it is written, man shall not live by bread alone, but by every word that proceedeth out of the mouth of God.

Using for subject, "*The Whole Counsel of God Must Be Represented.*" Every word is for everybody, and all views must be expressed, because conduct depends on the whole word of God: what is to be done, and what is not to be done. David could never have been a man after God's own heart if he didn't know what to cling to and what to avoid. Abraham could not have been a friend of God without knowing and without turning from that which was against the will of God.

It took counsel from Eli for Samuel to realize it was God calling, for at first Eli thought Samuel was calling him. And the virtuous woman could not have been virtuous unless she had received it from the Lord. They all had to know what was evil so they could turn from it, and what was good so they could hold fast to it.

For scripture tells us there was a man in the land of Uz, whose name is Job, and that man was perfect and upright, one who feared God and avoided evil. He had to know what evil was, to know it must be avoided, what it meant, and what came of it. For the whole counsel of God must be represented.

Moses told the children of Israel: *Therefore shall ye lay up these my words in your heart, the words God gave me to tell you—in your heart and in your soul. Bind them as a sign upon your hand, and let them be as frontlets between your eyes.* Not just the blessings, but the warnings too. Both what you should do and what you should not do must stay in remembrance.

And he saith, "Ye shall teach them to your children, speaking of them—"them" meaning the whole word of God—

when thou sittest in thine house, and when thou walkest by the way, when thou liest down, and when thou risest up.

God's word is not a fast-food restaurant, where you pick and choose from a menu. Every word is for me, whether I am doing it or not. For all the words of God must be sown in the hearts of man, so we may shun evil and cling to good.

The writer of Psalm 49 tells us where our trust should lie: Hear this, all ye people; give ear, all ye inhabitants of the world. If anyone does not take heed, the fault is not with the writer. For miracles were not only in the New Testament. Scripture shows how God used Elijah to bring the widow of Zarephath's son back to life. How Naaman dipped in the muddy Jordan seven times and was cleansed of leprosy. How a dead man revived when his body touched the bones of Elisha. How Daniel spent the night in the lions' den and was unharmed, for God shut the lions' mouths. And how three Hebrew boys, refusing to bow to Nebuchadnezzar's golden image, were thrown into the fiery furnace, yet came out without so much as the smell of smoke upon their clothes.

The psalmist lets us know this word is for everybody—godly and ungodly alike. The only ones fully mature in Christ are those who have passed on in Him; for us still living, there is learning yet to do. As Paul said, Not as though I had already attained, either were already perfect: but I follow after, if that I may apprehend that for which also I am apprehended of Christ Jesus.

I have heard people use the phrase, "You complete me." But if they are not talking about Christ, the picture is incomplete. For as long as we are in this mortal body, we have not reached the end. If it were otherwise, there would be no falling away, and scripture would not warn us: Now the Spirit speaketh expressly, that in the latter times some shall depart from the faith, giving heed to seducing spirits and doctrines of devils.

I remember when the church houses used to be full. Now it is every so often: you see me now, you don't. These are the times we live in. As the song saith, "If I never needed the Lord before, I sure do need him now."

I recall the Sunday after the storm Hugo. The church was packed so full, extra chairs had to be set in the aisles, and some even had to take detours to reach the house of the Lord. Something is going on now that is far worse than Hugo, and it is time to leave our own ways and turn to the way of God.

For the psalmist saith, *"Both low and high, rich and poor, together."* God's word is for all, no matter one's station in life. Attention and understanding must be applied, showing us where our trust should lie and what results will follow. We are warned not to set our hearts on what is seen, but on what is unseen. For what is seen is temporary, but what is unseen is eternal.

Riches may buy many things but not the redemption of a soul. Only God's will can secure that, when life is lived in right perspective according to His word. And as the psalmist says, this is for everybody to consider.

As in the parable of the sower, the seeds were not scattered only on ground expected to bear fruit. Every kind of ground was given a chance. As it has been said, If the Lord called me now, I had a chance. For the sower is Jesus, and the seed is the word of God.

But when the fowlers came, they devoured the seed. When the soil was shallow, the seed withered in the sun. For there is a way that seems right to man, but its end is death. The word may seem overwhelming; a blockade may rise up, and so the seed is taken away. God doesn't force himself on anybody, but he is there for the asking. for he said, *"Behold, I stand at the door and knock. If any man hears my voice and opens the door, I will come in and sup with him, and he with me."*

David said, *"Create in me a clean heart, O God, and renew a right spirit within me."* To stay within that prayer, the whole counsel of God must be represented, for the tree is known by the fruit it bears.

The sower didn't give up because some seed fell by the wayside. He kept on sowing. *Let us not be weary in well-doing, for in due season we shall reap if we faint not.*

Some seed fell on stony ground. It sprang up quickly, but withered because it had no root. Like the rich young ruler who asked Jesus, What good thing must I do to have eternal life? He practiced some parts, but when told to sell what he held back, he could not. The word was in him, but without root. For no man can serve two masters: he will love one and hate the other. As the saying goes, You can't have your cake and eat it too.

Still, the sower kept on sowing. Some seed fell among thorns. It took root, but bore no fruit, choked out by cares. For scripture says, *"Take no thought for your life, what ye shall eat or drink, nor yet for your body, what ye shall put on. Is not the life more than meat, and the body than raiment?"*

As Jesus told Martha, "Thou art careful and troubled about many things: but one thing is needful. And Mary hath chosen that good part, which shall not be taken away from her."

As David said, "One thing have I desire of the Lord, that I will seek after: that I may dwell in the house of the Lord all the days of my life, to behold the beauty of the Lord, and to inquire in his temple."

But when the word is choked by thorns, its powers is lost. Yet still I say, "Let us not be weary in well-doing, for payday is coming after a while."

For some seed fell on good ground. It took root, bore fruit, insight was given, and understanding was gained. It landed in the right heart.

After the resurrection of Jesus, scripture tells us He appeared again to the disciples by the sea of Tiberias. I can imagine how Peter felt—everything is all right now. You know how it is when you have been visited by Jesus.

For Peter said, "I go fishing." The others said, "We also go with thee." That night they caught nothing. But when the morning came—*weeping may endure for the night, but joy comes in the morning*—Jesus said, *"Cast the net on the right side of the ship, and ye shall find."*

And they did. Just as the seed that fell on good ground, the result was fruit. For *our conversation is in heaven; from whence we look for the Savior, the Lord Jesus Christ, who shall change our vile body, that it may be fashioned like unto His glorious* body.

As the butterfly didn't begin as a butterfly, but as a worm, so a metamorphosis must take place. A different outcome is possible when God works the change.

In this, we become the people of God, seeking first His kingdom and His righteousness, with His promise that He will supply all our needs according to His riches in glory. Still we are in the stage of transformation.

So, therefore, the whole counsel of God must be represented—the do's and the don'ts—in order to bring forth fruit that is acceptable. *He that hath ears to hear, let him hear.*

Topic: "The Result of Mismanagement"

Matthew 24:3-8

³And as he sat upon the mount of Olives, the disciples came unto him privately, saying, tell us, when shall these things be? And what shall be the sign of thy coming, and of the end of the world? ⁴And Jesus answered and said unto them, take heed that no man deceive you. ⁵For many shall come in my name, saying, I am Christ; and shall deceive many. ⁶And ye shall hear of wars and rumours of wars: see that ye be not troubled: for all these things must come to pass, but the end is not yet. ⁷For nation shall rise against nation, and kingdom against kingdom: and there shall be famines, and pestilences, and earthquakes, in divers places. ⁸All these are the beginning of sorrows.

1 John 2:15-19

¹⁵Love not the world, neither the things that are in the world. If any man love the world, the love of the Father is not in him. ¹⁶For all that is in the world, the lust of the flesh, and the lust of the eyes, and the pride of life, is not of the Father, but is of the world. ¹⁷And the world passeth away, and the lust thereof: but he that doeth the will of God abideth for ever. ¹⁸Little children, it is the last time: and as ye have heard that

antichrist shall come, even now are there many antichrists; whereby we know that it is the last time. [19]They went out from us, but they were not of us; for if they had been of us, they would no doubt have continued with us: but they went out, that they might be made manifest that they were not all of us.

These scriptures are letting us know that the world as we know it is coming to an end.

Using a subject, *"The Result of Mismanagement,"* for God created a peaceful habitation, and this is the result of what is contrary. For the scriptures let us know, ye are blessed by the Lord which made heaven and earth. The heavens, even the heavens, are the Lord's, but the earth hath he given to the children of men. And it also tells us, thou hast made him a little lower than the angels and hast crowned him with glory and honor. Thou madest him to have dominion over the works of thy hands; thou hast put all things under his feet. The question is, did man rule on God's behalf? The answer is no; we did not. But thank God for another chance, one that was rejected by many.

And therefore, the result is this: as he sat upon the Mount of Olives, the disciples came unto him privately, saying, tell us, when shall these things be? And what shall be the sign of thy coming and of the end of the world? The angel Gabriel told Daniel in so many words that this would come to pass: to stop people from turning against God, to put an end to sin, to take away evil, to bring in goodness that continues forever, to make the vision and prophecy come true, and to appoint a most holy place. I can understand why Daniel kept on praying while told not to. And why the Hebrew boys refused to bow down to King Nebuchadnezzar golden image.

As I heard one preach: to be ready is good, but they were staying ready. There is a song that saith, my Lord is getting us ready for that great day. And for those in the will of God, it will be a great day, for those who shall be able to stand.

Those, Jesus said, that do the will of my father in heaven. And Jesus answered, saying, "Take heed that no man deceives you." For he has provided everything needed to maintain faithfulness. Not only that, but he is also on the inside, working on the outside to keep in place the requirements of a godly life. So when the deceiver comes, we can say as Job said, "God forbid that I should justify you; until I die, I will not remove mine integrity from me. My righteousness I hold fast, and I will not let it go; my heart shall not reproach me as long as I live. And as Paul said, herein do I exercise myself, to always have a conscience void of offense toward God and toward men."

For there are those who don't want God for themselves and don't want you to have him either. For many shall come in my name, saying, I am Christ, and shall deceive many, telling us there will be pretenders in the last days. For the scripture lets us know, this same Jesus which was taken up from you into heaven shall so come in like manner as ye have seen him go. Therefore, where is your mighty angel, where is your smoke, and where is your fire if ye be the Christ? Then bring about the purpose of what shall be.

Then he let us know: *ye shall hear of wars and rumors of wars; see that ye be not troubled, for all these things must come to pass, but the end is not yet.* Still time to get one's house in order. Still time to cry out to Jesus. As a certain ruler asked, good master, what shall I do to inherit eternal life? Still time to tell somebody what they must do to inherit eternal life. Not only should we want God for ourselves, but we should want him for everybody else.

For nations shall rise against nations, and there shall be famines, pestilence, and earthquakes in many places. All these are the beginning of sorrow. But the scriptures give us consolation, as the song saith, *soul, let the train run easy. Soul, I am resting in Jesus, God going to do just what he says.* For our light affliction, which is just for a moment, worketh for us a far more exceeding and eternal weight of glory, and that glory is greater than our troubles. While we look not at the things which are seen but at the things which are not seen—for the things which are seen are temporary, but the things which are not seen are eternal.

If one says there are no troubles in our lives, we are also saying there is no Jesus in our lives, for he saith, take up your cross daily and follow me. And it also tells us, if we suffer with him, we shall also reign with him; if we deny him, he also will deny us. One doesn't have to say I deny Jesus with words from the mouth, but by not doing what he said.

When David said, "I was glad when they said unto me, let us go into the house of the Lord," it may be because he had been through something and needed relief. As Hezekiah did when trouble came his way—he went to the house of the Lord. He is saying, if one never goes through anything, they are not about anything. For that kind of life is only in fiction books, an imaginary thing with imaginary people. But in the real world, part of glorifying is saying, "I have been through this, I have been through that, and the Lord brought me out of them all."

For when there are no challenges in one's life, life becomes mundane, dull, without meaningful purpose. And we see it on the news every day, the result of mismanagement, for God created a peaceful habitation.

Verse 10: *And then shall many be offended, and shall betray one another, and shall hate one another.* The many are those who once believed but lost their faith. They do not have the steadfastness of Paul, who said, *To live is Christ,* as long as I remain in this mortal body dedicated to Him. *O death, where is thy sting? O grave, where is thy victory?* Mission accomplished. Starting is good, but finishing is better. And many false prophets shall rise and shall deceive many.

We live in a world where people prefer the easy way out, but easy doesn't always mean better. Test the spirit, by the Spirit, to see whether it is of God. And because sin will increase, the love of many will grow cold. There is even a song that says, What's love got to do with it? I can be with you and you with me, without love being involved. But not so with Jesus, for where there is no love, there is no Christ. When love stops, a right relationship with God is stops, for love is the bond of perfection. Scripture tells us, Be ye therefore perfect, even as your father which is in Heaven is perfect.

But he that endures to the end shall be saved. I once heard someone say, "I am in it for the long haul. If I get to a place where I cannot walk, I will drag myself." For Jesus said, Be thou faithful unto death, and I will give thee a crown of life. Hold on and hold out, for a better day is coming, by and by, for those who are born again—with the hope that when we look for others, they too will be there.

Jesus knew he was going to raise Lazarus from the dead back to earthly life. Yet Mary said to Him, I know that he shall rise again in the resurrection at the last day. It is good to live for Jesus in this life, but the best life is the one with Him in the resurrection. Behold, the tabernacle of God is with men, and He will dwell with them, and they shall be His people, and God Himself shall be with them, and be their God. And God shall wipe away all tears from their eyes; there shall be no more death, nor sorrow, nor crying, nor pain, for the former things have passed away. For his words are true and faithful.

Therefore, those on the outside still have a chance to be on the inside, because Jesus said, This gospel of the kingdom shall be preached in all the world for a witness unto all nations, and then shall the end come. Giving us all a chance to make our calling sure. For He also said, All that call upon Me shall not enter into my rest.

Therefore, as God sent word by Isaiah to tell Hezekiah, *"Set thine house in order, for thou shalt die. And like the young man who said to Jesus, All these things have I kept from my youth up; what lack I yet?"* —we are reminded that as long as we live in this flesh, there are still things we must strive for. As Paul said, Not as though I had already attained, either were already perfect; but I follow after, if that I may apprehend that for which also I am apprehended of Jesus Christ.

Not ready yet as God wants me to be, for there is still more to fulfill. As scripture tells us, The earth hath He given to the children of men. And it is in this condition because of mismanagement—mismanagement that can also happen in our walk with God if we allow other interests to take precedence.

I remember while picking cotton in a field near a house, the wife came out and told her husband there was no meal in the house. He said he didn't care whether there was meal or not, but when it was time to eat, he wanted to eat. But if we hold the wrong perspective, there will be no eating at God's banquet table.

For 1 John tells us, *"Love not the world, neither the things that are in the world. If any man love the world, the love of the Father is not in him."* For the love of the world is contrary to the will of God, and the two cannot go together. For all that is in the world—the lust of the flesh, the lust of the eyes, and the pride of life—is not of the Father but is of the world.

Remember the man with the bigger barns, who thought he was set for life. But God said unto him, *Thou fool, this night thy soul shall be required of thee.* Letting us know that there is no time left for validation or delay. No one is set for life without the involvement of Jesus Christ. No Jesus, no security.

Then it reminds us, *The world passeth away, and the lust thereof: but he that doeth the will of God abideth forever.* Only those born again—not of corruptible seed but incorruptible, by the word of God which lives and abides forever—shall stand.

Little children, it is the last time: and as ye have heard that antichrist shall come, even now there are many antichrists; whereby we know it is the last time. So study to show yourself approved, rightly dividing the word of truth. Truth always rises to the top. And again, we are told: try the spirit by the Spirit, to see whether it is of God.

They went out from us, but they were not of us; for if they had been of us, they would no doubt have continued with us: but they went out, that they might be made manifest that they were not of us.

There is a saying: If you cannot stand the heat, get out of the kitchen. And another: May the life I live speak for me—and it will. No matter what that life looks like, for Jesus said, *All that the Father giveth Me shall come to Me; and him that cometh to Me I will in no wise cast out.* Safe and secure from all alarm.

And the result? Be esteemed, for God will do just what he said. *He that acknowledges the son hath the father also.* If you know He is righteous, then you know that everyone who practices righteousness is born of Him.

Behold, what manner of love the Father hath bestowed upon us, that we should be called the sons of God. And it does not yet appear what we shall be: but we know that, when He shall appear, we shall be like Him, for we shall see Him as He is. No longer looking through a glass darkly, but then face to face.

Topic: "Becoming A Professional"

James 1:12-18

[12]Blessed is the man that endureth temptation: for when he is tried, he shall receive the crown of life, which the Lord hath promised to them that love him. [13]Let no man say when he is tempted, I am tempted of God: for God cannot be tempted with evil, neither tempteth he any man: [14]But every man is tempted, when he is drawn away of his own lust, and enticed. [15]Then when lust hath conceived, it bringeth forth sin: and sin, when it is finished, bringeth forth death. [16]Do not err, my beloved brethren.[17]Every good gift and every perfect gift is from above, and cometh down from the Father of lights, with whom is no variableness, neither shadow of turning. [18]Of his own will begat he us with the word of truth, that we should be a kind of firstfruits of his creatures.

Philippian 3:12-16

[12]Not as though I had already attained, either were already perfect: but I follow after, if that I may apprehend that for which also I am apprehended of Christ Jesus. [13]Brethren, I count not myself to have apprehended: but this one thing I do, forgetting those things which are behind, and reaching forth unto those things which are before, [14]I press toward the mark for the prize of the high calling of God in Christ Jesus. [15]Let us therefore, as many as be perfect, be thus minded: and if in

any thing ye be otherwise minded, God shall reveal even this unto you. [16]Nevertheless, whereto we have already attained, let us walk by the same rule, let us mind the same thing.

Using for a subject; *"Becoming A Professional"* Engaged in a specified activity as one's main occupation. There is a certain involvement that must take place, not just hearing the word, but doing it, for the word tells us to work out our own salvation. Just as there is work to supply our physical needs, there is also work to supply our spiritual needs.

Proverbs tells us, *"Train up a child in the way he should go, and when he is old, he will not depart from it."* In the same way, train up a Christian so they may not depart, and that is done by the complete word of God.

Preparation is needed for both the physical and the spiritual. Sometimes in the natural, a part-time job can meet a person's needs. But not in the spiritual—it's either all the way or none of the way, for it is an ongoing process, a lifetime commitment. As Isaiah said, "In the year that King Uzziah died, I saw also the Lord sitting upon a throne, high and lifted up, and his train filled the temple." His training must fill the heart, a heart willing to accept detailed supervision. Not like the prophet from Judah, whom God sent on a mission to warn Jeroboam. His charge from God was, Eat no bread, drink no water, and do not return by the same way you came. For scripture tells us, There is a way that seems right unto a man, but the end thereof is the way of death.

There was a song that saith, "I did it my way," but in this man's case, God's way was the best. There is a process we must undergo to reach the spiritual state required by God. Scripture tells us, *"Be ye steadfast, unmovable, always abounding in the work of the Lord; for as much as ye know that your labor is not in vain in the Lord."*

Some days when I don't feel like it, I say to myself, "I am not going to that sewing machine today." But I never say, "I am not going to the Lord today." For this is not like the marriage vows that sayeth, "Till death do us part." Often, death is the judgment, and I don't want to be like the five foolish virgins who were not there when the bridegroom came and the door was shut. But thanks be to God, who provides us the victory through our Lord Jesus Christ. For I can say with David, "A day in thy courts is better than a thousand. I had rather be a doorkeeper in the house of my God than dwell in the tents of wickedness. For the Lord will give grace and glory. No good thing will he withhold from them that walk uprightly."

As he said unto Abram, before his name was changed to Abraham: I am thy shield and thy exceeding great reward. The is the result of participating in the will of God. For James tells us, Blessed is the man that endureth temptation; for when he is tried, he shall receive the crown of life, which the Lord hath promised to them that love him. Love for God is a shield. It blocks out what is contrary and makes room for what is acceptable. And so it is written: When thou passest through the waters, I will be with thee; and through the rivers, they shall not overflow thee. When thou walkest through the fire, thou shalt not be burned, neither shall the flame kindle upon thee.

Love for God surrounds us, not stopping the trials of the natural, but keeping us through them. Scripture tells us, *If we suffer, we shall also reign with him; if we deny him, he will also deny us.* But through this, we are spiritually perfected, able to live blameless in moral behavior. As the song says, *Let nobody turn you around, keep on marching to Galilee.* So when the hellhounds come knocking, we can say, "Get thee behind me, Satan," and they will flee.

And when Jesus appears again, it will be proven that greater is he that is in me than he that is in the world. For the joy of the Lord is my strength. When I was a child, I used to wish I had not been born, so I would not have to die. But scripture showed me: To be absent from the body is to be present with the Lord. O death, where is thy sting? Oh grave, where is thy victory?

As Jesus said unto Martha, "*I am the resurrection and the life. He that believeth in me, though he were dead, yet shall he live. For death is only a passing—from this life into the next. And the book of James tells us: Let no man say when he is tempted, I am tempted of God. For God cannot be tempted with evil, neither tempteth he any man. But every man is tempted when he is drawn away by his own lust and enticed.*"

God draws us to Him—He does not lead us astray. When God says "do," and a man lets another source stop him from applying it, the fault lies with the man, for he has turned from what is genuine. *Greater is he that is in me than he that is in the world.* To be enticed by what is contrary creates a false balance, and scripture tells us, "*A false balance is abomination to the Lord, but a just weight is his delight.*"

As the saying goes, "You can't have your cake and eat it too. If you eat it, you no longer have it. So the things I used to do, I don't do anymore. No more deeds of sin, but alive to God. Not another chance to say, "I want to be in the number one more time." No nearer to God to say, What shall separate me from the love of Christ? Having been freed from sin, to return to it is a dangerous thing. For verse 16 warns: Do not err, my beloved brethren.

I have heard people say, "I gave up the chance of a lifetime," something they could have done to make a better life. But James warns us not to give up the life that comes after this one. Every good and perfect gift is from above, and comes down from the Father of lights, with whom there is no variableness, neither shadow of turning. For God is not a man that He should lie. If He has spoken, He will make it good..

So I say to my soul: let the train run easy, for God will do what He has said. We can rest in that assurance. As the saying goes—you can take it to the bank. As David said, *"Thy word is a lamp unto my feet, and a light unto my path."*

Verse 18 tells us: *Of His own will begat He us with the word of truth, that we should be a kind of firstfruits of His creation.* Showing us the kind of life we should live. Two of John's disciples looked upon Jesus as He walked. John said, *Behold the Lamb of God.* And the two disciples heard him speak and followed Jesus. Then Jesus turned and saw them following, and said, *"What seek ye?"* They said, *"Rabbi, where dwellest thou?"* He answered, *"Come and see."*

We must live a "come and see" life in order to be the firstfruits of his creation. No longer navigating our own life but under the management of Almighty God. As the song saith, "My soul is anchored in the Lord."

This what it takes to become as Jesus said: Be ye perfect, even as I am perfect. Life is an ongoing process. Where I am today, I will not be tomorrow, for I am moving forward in the word of God. As Paul told Timothy, Study to show thyself approved, rightly dividing the word of truth.

In other words, do not remain still. As Paul said, "Not as though I had already attained, either were already perfect; but I follow after, if that I may apprehend that for which also I am apprehended of Christ Jesus. All that I know now is not all that can be known, and I want it all. For in this life, there is no room for what is contrary, it only blocks what should be."

Brethren, I count not myself to have apprehended: but this one thing I do—forgiving those things which are behind, and reaching forth unto those things which are before. As Jesus said, No man, having put his hand to the plow, and looking back, is fit for the kingdom of God.

"Therefore," Paul said, "I press toward the mark for the prize of the high calling of God in Christ Jesus." No standing still. There is always more than what I have now, and I want that too. *Let us therefore, as many as be perfect, be thus minded: and if in anything ye be otherwise minded, God shall reveal even this unto you.*

Live according to the truth you have already attained, and what else you need to know, God will reveal. For he will supply all our needs according to his riches in glory. *Nevertheless, whereto we have already attained, let us walk by the same rule, let us mind the same thing.*

So let us live by the truth we have attained, trusting God to reveal the rest. And then we can do as the song saith, "I lift your name on high," and when you lift his name on high, it makes you feel good in your satisfied soul.

Topic: "That which was Intended for Evil, God Turn it Into Good"

Genesis 37:5-8

⁵And Joseph dreamed a dream, and he told it his brethren: and they hated him yet more. ⁶And he said unto them, hear, I pray you, this dream which I have dreamed: ⁷for behold, we were binding sheaves in the field, and lo, my sheaf arose, and also stood upright; and behold, your sheaves stood round about, and made obeisance to my sheaf. ⁸And his brethren said to him, shalt thou indeed reign over us? Or shalt thou indeed have dominion over us? And they hated him yet the more for his dreams, and for his words.

Genesis 37:23-28

²³And it came to pass, when Joseph was come unto his brethren, that they stript Joseph out of his coat, his coat of many colors that was on him; ²⁴and they took him and cast him into a pit; and the pit was empty, there was no water in it. ²⁵And they sat down to eat bread: and they lifted up their eyes and looked, and behold, a company of Ishmaelites came from Gilead with their camels bearing spicery and balm and myrrh, going to carry it down to Egypt. ²⁶And Judah said unto his brethren, what profit is it if we slay our brother, and conceal his blood? ²⁷Come, and let us sell him to the Ishmaelites, and

let not our hand be upon him; for he is our brother and our flesh. And his brethren were content. [28]Then there passed by Midianites merchantmen; and they drew and lifted up Joseph out of the pit and sold Joseph to the Ishmaelites for twenty pieces of silver: and they brought Joseph into Egypt.

Using as a topic, *"That which was Intended for Evil, God Turn it Into Good."* For the Lord saith, *"My thoughts are not your thoughts, neither are your ways My ways. For as the heavens are higher than the earth, so are My ways higher than your ways, and My thoughts than your thoughts."* This tells us that man's view of how things should be done is not the same as God's without His insight. God's perspective is always to bring about good, not evil. And this message is about whose thoughts prevail—God's or man's—for all failure comes from man's side. For Jesus said, *"Of them which Thou gavest Me have I lost none."* That shows us plainly: when man's thoughts clash with God's, there is no question who will come out the loser.

It also teaches us not to prefer one child over another, for that breeds jealousy. Joseph was the firstborn son of Rachel, and perhaps his father's love for Rachel clouded his judgment. He favored Joseph, just as favoritism had marked his own life. Perhaps you have heard the saying, "What goes around, comes around." meaning you will see it again. For the scripture tells us: Joseph dreamed a dream, and when he shared it, his brothers hated him all the more. The hate was already there; the dream only added fuel. Joseph said unto them, "Hear, I pray you, this dream which I have dreamed: for behold, we were binding sheaves in the field, and lo, my sheaf arose and stood upright; and behold, your sheaves stood round about and bowed down to mine." He did not know that this day would come to pass. But there is a time to speak and a time to keep silent, for only God knows the future.

James warns us, "Ye that say, Today or tomorrow we will go into such a city and continue there a year, and buy and sell, and get gain; whereas ye know not what shall be on the morrow. For what is your life? It is even a vapor, that appears for a little time, and then vanishes away. For that ye ought to say, If the Lord will, we shall live, and do this, or that." But Joseph's brothers said instead, "Shalt thou indeed reign over us? Shalt thou indeed have dominion?" And they hated him yet the more for his dreams and for his words. Not knowing that hate harms the hater more than the hated. For hate, as the old saying goes, breaks down the wagon and keeps a soul from moving forward in the goodness of life God has provided.

Scripture says, "*It came to pass, when Joseph was come unto his brethren, that they stripped him out of his coat, his coat of many colors that was on him.*" I believe Joseph loved that coat. He took pride in it, maybe thinking nothing bad could touch him while he wore it. But Jesus said, "*Whosoever shall exalt himself shall be humbled, and he that humbleth himself shall be exalted.*" Joseph was not only a victim here; some of it he brought on by his own pride. Like any family of children, quarrels and accusations stirred things up, until at last they cast him into a pit—an empty cistern where no water was. This shows us God's timing is always right. Suffering, like everything else in life, has its purpose.

Jacob's favorite son must have felt abandoned, hearing his brothers laugh and eat together while he sat alone in the pit. Yet this suffering was part of God's preparation for what Joseph would one day do. Growing pains had to come. Then a company of Ishmaelites passed by, bound for Egypt. His brothers chose the lesser of two evils: they would sell him instead of kill him. Proverbs says of the adulterous woman, "*She eats, and wipes her mouth, and says, I have done no wickedness.*" They excused themselves, but they did not yet see God's hand in what was unfolding. For Joseph in Egypt was God's plan—not only for Joseph's good but for theirs also. Judah said, *"Come, let us sell him to the Ishmaelites, and let not our hand be upon him, for he is our brother and our flesh."* And they were content.

But scripture later tells us that God himself called for a famine in the land. He broke the whole staff of bread. Yet He had already sent a man before them: Joseph, sold as a servant. His feet were hurt with fetters, his soul tested in irons, until the appointed time came. Then the word of the Lord proved true. The king sent and loosed him, made him master of the house, ruler of all substance, to bind princes at his will and teach senators wisdom. This same Joseph, sold for twenty pieces of silver, was raised up by God. What was meant for evil, God turned into good.

God delivered him from affliction but did not stop there. For when something is taken away, God provides something greater in its place. He gave Joseph wisdom and favor in Pharaoh's sight, making him governor of Egypt. From the pit to the palace—for God was with him. And when God is for us, who can be against us?

Joseph opened the storehouses of Egypt to save lives in famine. Many have said Joseph was a type of Christ. In his day, men went to Joseph for bread that sustained the body. But for eternal life, we go to Jesus, who gives bread from heaven. Joseph could prevent starvation, but only Christ can prevent damnation. For He said, *"Labor not for the meat which perisheth, but for that meat which endureth unto everlasting life, which the Son of man shall give unto you: for Him hath God the Father* sealed."

You can't obtain this with your hands, for it must come through the heart—not by physical labor, but by a transformation of the heart. For He did what the bread of Joseph could not do. That which is of the earth is earthly, and its means are earthly, for the purpose of earthly life. But for eternal life, there is that which beans and peas cannot provide. You don't need to eat every edible food to survive, but it is not so with the bread of God, which comes down from heaven and gives life to the world—it is essential. Some may claim to be vegetarians, but in the Word of God, there is no picking and choosing, taking some and leaving others. Man must live by every word that proceeds from the mouth of God.

It is said that certain foods are essential for the health of the body, but every word from the mouth of God is essential for the saving of the soul. This did not come by the one who was sold for twenty pieces of silver and carried into Egypt, but by the One spoken of by the prophet: "Out of Egypt have I called my son," for his son was like no other son. All others were conceived by two, but he was conceived by the Holy Ghost for the saving of mankind from our sins.

Joseph, the son of Jacob, gave food for physical life. But God's son is the food for everlasting life. For the Scripture says, "My God shall supply all your needs according to His riches in glory." Perhaps He is not coming back from glory to hand out one piece of bread, but He has provided a ram in the bush, as He said to Abraham: "Take now thy son, thine only son Isaac, whom thou lovest, and get thee into the land of Moriah and offer him there for a burnt offering upon one of the mountains which I will tell thee of." But before the knife in his hand touched his son, an angel of the Lord called out from heaven, saying, "Lay not thy hand upon the lad." For all God wanted was proof of evidence—that one's commitment to Him was tested, tried, and true, that nothing in life came before God.

The ram in the bush is symbolic of God not withholding any good thing from those who love him and keep his commandments. For it is said, "God so loved the world that He gave"—gave meaning He died, that man might live. Joseph was sold for twenty pieces of silver; Judas Iscariot sold Jesus for thirty pieces of silver—more value placed on the soul than the body. For the body returns to the dust from which it came, but the soul returns to God who gave it. And where it goes from there depends on our earthly commitment.

That is why I sing, "I'm going to do what the Lord saith to do. For upon this rock I stand; all other ground is sinking sand." For as famine covered the face of the earth, Joseph opened all the storehouses. And when sin covered the earth, God opened salvation, saying, "Whosoever will, let them come."

Sermon: "A Promise Kept"

Deuteronomy 18:15-19

[15]The LORD thy God will raise up unto thee a Prophet from the midst of thee, of thy brethren, like unto me; unto him ye shall hearken; [16]According to all that thou desiredst of the LORD thy God in Horeb in the day of the assembly, saying, Let me not hear again the voice of the LORD my God, neither let me see this great fire any more, that I die not. [17]And the LORD said unto me, They have well spoken that which they have spoken. [18]I will raise them up a Prophet from among their brethren, like unto thee, and will put my words in his mouth; and he shall speak unto them all that I shall command him. [19]And it shall come to pass, that whosoever will not hearken unto my words which he shall speak in my name, I will require it of him.

John 3:16-20

[16]For God so loved the world, that he gave his only begotten Son, that whosoever believeth in him should not perish, but have everlasting life. [17]For God sent not his Son into the world to condemn the world; but that the world through him might be saved. [18]He that believeth on him is not condemned: but he that believeth not is condemned already, because he hath not believed in the name of the only begotten Son of God. [19]And this is the condemnation, that light is come into the

world, and men loved darkness rather than light, because their deeds were evil. [20]For every one that doeth evil hateth the light, neither cometh to the light, lest his deeds should be reproved.

Using for a subject: "*A Promise Kept.*" Staying the way it was said, no changing of the mind in the circumstances as stated; this is the way it is and will be. His commitment will be fulfilled. As the saying goes, "God said it, I believe it, and I'm going to take him at his word."

Last Christmas, the message was about the birth of Jesus, titled "The Gift That Keeps on Giving." This time, it's not manager talk, but his purpose for being born into the world. For the Scripture tells us in Isaiah 6:10: "*Make the heart of this people fat, and make their ears heavy, and shut their eyes; lest they see with their eyes, and hear with their ears, and understand with their heart, and convert, and be healed.*" A right relationship with the Lord is not a casual thing; it is a total commitment. Scripture tells us: "*Let your light so shine before men, that they may see your good works and glorify your Father which is in heaven.*" That becomes a road map for someone else to follow.

There is a great divide between the children of God and those who are not. No part of their lifestyle should be self-made. Moses said unto the children of Israel: these nations you will possess listen to fortune-tellers and diviners, but as for you, the Lord your God has not allowed you to do so. A right relationship with the Lord is not mass-produced like something from a machine. One doesn't have to follow what others do. That's why King Agrippa could say unto Paul, "Almost thou persuadest me to be a Christian." For the Scripture tells us, "Let this mind be in you, which was also in Christ Jesus." When decision time comes, the right thing will appear.

Moses told the people, "The Lord thy God will raise up unto thee a Prophet from the midst of thee, of thy brethren, like unto me; unto him ye shall hearken." This is the one Philip told Nathanael about: "We have found him, of whom Moses in the law, and the prophets, did write—Jesus of Nazareth, the son of Joseph." But more importantly, the son of God.

Exodus tells us when the people saw Moses delayed coming down from the mountain, they gathered around Aaron and said, "Make us gods to go before us. For this Moses, the man who brought us out of Egypt, we don't know what has become of him." They wanted a god they could see. Jesus is the God we can see. Before returning to His Father, He said, *"Yet a little while, and the world seeth me no more; but ye see me: because I live, ye shall live also."* I see Him every day, not with physical eyes but with spiritual insight.

Then the Scripture saith, "According to all that thou *desiredst of the Lord thy God in Horeb in the day of the assembly, saying, Let me not hear again the voice of the Lord my God, neither let me see this great fire any more, that I die not."* Perhaps you've heard the phrase "too hot to handle"—the way God appeared with thundering, lightning, trumpet sounds, and the smoking mountain. The people said to Moses: *"You speak with us and we will hear, but let not God speak with us, lest we die."* Jesus is our go-between. He speaks to the Father on our behalf: *"Father, forgive them; for they know not what they do."* He sits at the right hand of God, making intercession for us.

Verse 17 says, "And the Lord said unto me, They have well spoken." They confessed they needed a go-between. King Jesus is that go-between, for He said: *"I am the way, the truth, and the life: no man cometh unto the Father but* by me. Since the direct word from God was too much for them to bear, God promised, *"I will raise them up a Prophet from among their brethren, like unto thee, and will put my words in his mouth; and he shall speak unto them all that I shall command him."*

Jesus is that Prophet. He declared, *"Man shall not live by bread alone, but by every word that proceedeth out of the mouth of God."* Tell them, Jesus. *"He that findeth his life shall lose it: and he that loseth his life for my sake shall find it."* *"Blessed are the poor in spirit: for theirs is the kingdom of heaven."* Tell them, Jesus. *"A new commandment I give unto you, That ye love one another; as I have loved you, that ye also love one another."*

No longer the old self, but a new creation in Christ Jesus. As the song saith, "The things I used to do, I don't do them anymore." For what is born of the flesh is flesh, and what is born of the Spirit is spirit. The woman at the well said to Him, "I know that Messiah cometh, which is called Christ: when he is come, he will tell us all things." It is good to know what Scripture says, but even better to live it.

For God said, "It shall come to pass, that whatsoever will not hearken unto my words which he shall speak in my name, I will require it of him." This is the greatest loss of all—to be cut off from the will of God. No days off from walking with Him. As in the parable of the five foolish virgins, you must be ready at all times. David said: *"For a day in thy courts is better than a thousand. I had rather be a doorkeeper in the house of my God, than to dwell in the tents of wickedness."*

After all God has done for the sake of mankind, as the song saith, "I want to be in the number, one more time." Not just once, but at all times. For God so loved the world that He gave His only begotten Son, that whosoever believes in Him should not perish but have everlasting life. What a mighty God we serve! *"But God commendeth his love toward us, in that, while we were yet sinners, Christ died for us."* The church needs to shout glory.

The angels sang, "Glory to the newborn King," the beginning of the reuniting of God and man. For God sent not His Son into the world to condemn the world, but that the world through Him might be saved. His love goes beyond human understanding. Innocent blood was shed so that we might take on the righteousness of God. For *"He was wounded for our transgressions, bruised for our iniquities: the chastisement of our peace was upon him; and with is stripes we are healed."*

All that remains is to grow in grace and in the knowledge of our Lord and Savior Jesus Christ. As Paul said: *"I count not myself to have apprehended: but this one thing I do, forgetting those things which are behind, and reaching forth unto those things which are before."* Pressing toward the mark for the prize of the high calling of God in Christ Jesus, chasing after Jesus.

When the Samaritans would not receive him, James and John asked, "Lord, should we call down fire from heaven to consume them, as Elijah did?" But He told them: *"The Son of man is not come to destroy men's lives, but to save them."*. A long time ago the Lord asked me what I want. I said I want others to be saved; you see, you can't have salvation for yourself without wanting it for somebody else.

Verse 18 tells us: *"He that believeth on him is not condemned: but he that believeth not is condemned already."* Just as there was no mood swing in Christ, there cannot be in us. He said: *"Take up your cross daily, and follow me."* Following Jesus is not a work week—five days on, two days off. It is an all-time thing.

And the result? As Jesus said, *"He that heareth my word, and believeth on him that sent me, hath everlasting life, and shall not come into condemnation; but is passed from death unto life."* Who wouldn't want that?

And this is the condemnations: light has come into the world, but men loved darkness rather than light because their deeds were evil. Yet Jesus is the antidote, the only medicine that heals the soul. He removes what should not be and replaces it with what should.

"For everyone that doeth evil hateth the light, neither cometh to the light, lest his deeds should be reproved." My deeds have been reproved. I am no longer the old self but a new creation in Christ Jesus. No lights in my windows, but light in my heart. And often I ask the Lord, "If there is anything in me not of you, take it away."

What a Christmas it is to be in the right relationship with the Lord. For He said, *"Be ye perfect, even as your Father in heaven is perfect."* God never commands without giving the ability to fulfill. The gifts of man are temporary, but the gift He gives is eternal; the gates of hell cannot prevail against it.

That's what God said, and I am going to take him at his word. And the result is to grow in grace and in the knowledge of our Lord and Savior Jesus Christ. Blessed in the Lord! For the Scripture saith, "Who shall separate us from the love of Christ?" Then it lists all that cannot: tribulations, distress, persecution, famine, or nakedness. And it lists what does happen because of our walk with Christ: *"For thy sake we are killed all the day long; we are accounted as sheep for the slaughter."*

But in all these things we are more than conquerors through him who loved us. Paul said, "I am persuaded, that neither death, nor life, nor angels, nor principalities, nor powers, nor any other creature, shall be able to separate us from the love of God, which is in Christ Jesus."

The only separation possible is from me, myself, and I. And I am not going to do that.

Subject: "Being of the Wrong Expectation"

2 Samuel 1:1-11

¹Now it came to pass after the death of Saul, when David was returned from the slaughter of the Amalekites, and David had abode two days in Ziklag; ²It came even to pass on the third day, that, behold, a man came out of the camp from Saul with his clothes rent, and earth upon his head: and so it was, when he came to David, that he fell to the earth, and did obeisance. ³And David said unto him, From whence comest thou? And he said unto him, Out of the camp of Israel am I escaped. ⁴And David said unto him, How went the matter? I pray thee, tell me. And he answered, That the people are fled from the battle, and many of the people also are fallen and dead; and Saul and Jonathan his son are dead also. ⁵And David said unto the young man that told him, How knowest thou that Saul and Jonathan his son be dead? ⁶And the young man that told him said, As I happened by chance upon mount Gilboa, behold, Saul leaned upon his spear; and, lo, the chariots and horsemen followed hard after him. ⁷And when he looked behind him, he saw me, and called unto me. And I answered, Here am I. ⁸And he said unto me, Who art thou? And I answered him, I am an Amalekite. ⁹He said unto me again, Stand, I pray thee, upon me, and slay me: for anguish

is come upon me, because my life is yet whole in me. [10]So I stood upon him, and slew him, because I was sure that he could not live after that he was fallen: and I took the crown that was upon his head, and the bracelet that was on his arm, and have brought them hither unto my lord. [11]Then David took hold on his clothes, and rent them; and likewise all the men that were with him:

Using for a subject, *"Being of the Wrong Expectation."* Thinking things would happen one way, but they turned out another. Not going as one had hoped. Believing he had a message that would please David. What was he thinking being one of the very people God told Israel to utterly destroy? One of the ones David had just returned from defeating. Yet he thought he had a message David would welcome, even a reward. For the scripture says he fell to the earth and did obeisance, acting as if he were grieving over the matter. But the word reminds us that a double-minded man is unstable in all his ways.

It came to pass on the third day that a man came out of Saul's camp with torn clothes and earth upon his head; when he came to David, he fell to the ground in respect, as if he were deeply troubled. But in his heart he thought he was bringing David good news — that his enemy was dead. Yet the teaching is clear: love your enemies, bless those who curse you, do good to those who hate you, and pray for those who mistreat and persecute you. He thought David would feel relief at Saul's death, but instead David held fast to a different standard: "Do unto others as you would have them do unto you," whether they return it or not. That was David's way.

So David said unto him, "From whence cometh thou?" And he answered, "Out of the camp of Israel am I escaped."

Then David asked, "How went the matter? I pray thee, tell me."

He replied, "The people are fled from the battle, and many are fallen and dead; and Saul and Jonathan his son are dead also." Thus began his false confession. But what he didn't know was that a false confession brings about a false result. Expecting one thing and receiving another, for a false balance is an abomination to the Lord, but a just weight is his delight.

The man claimed, "As I came upon Mount Gilboa, I saw Saul leaning on his spear, with chariots and horsemen pressing hard after him. He looked back, saw me, and called to me. I answered, 'Here am I.'" My mother used to say, when you tell one lie, you must tell another to back it up. So he went on, asking Saul who he was, and he answered, "I am an Amalekite," one of the very people God had ordered Saul to destroy. He spun out the tale, but the truth had already been recorded: Saul's death was not by his hand, and nothing could change that. As Paul said, "Study to show thyself approved, rightly dividing the word of truth." It is never wise to claim credit for something you didn't do.

The Amalekite thought his words would bring David joy and reward. Instead, they brought grief and lamentation for Saul and Jonathan, his son. A false confession brought about a false result, expecting praise but finding death. For David called one of his young men and said, "Go near, and fall upon him." And the man struck him, so that he died.

He stood no chance with David, but he still had a chance with Jesus. For Jesus said, "The Spirit of the Lord is upon me, because he has anointed me to bring good news to the poor, to heal the brokenhearted, to proclaim deliverance to the captives." After his crucifixion and before his resurrection, he preached to those who had died outside salvation, giving them the invitation: "Whosoever will, let them come."

For it is written: "Thou wilt not leave my soul in hell, neither wilt thou suffer thine Holy One to see corruption." The gospel was preached even to the dead, that they might be judged according to men in the flesh, but live according to God in the spirit. This was a one-time act to set captives free, showing that nothing in mankind is beyond His power to restore.

Jesus proved it when he said to the man with the withered hand, "Stretch forth your hand." And he stretched it out, and it was made whole like the other. Life outside of Christ is incomplete; he is not like life insurance, "better to have it and not need it." Without him, there is no life at all. He is Lord of the natural and the supernatural. No place exists where Jesus is not already there.

David once asked, "Where can I go from Your presence?" and named many places, but God was already in them all. The Amalekite and Jesus had one thing in common: both died for things they did not do. The difference, as Peter wrote, is this: "Christ also hath once suffered for sins, the just for the unjust, that he might bring us to God."

There are many invitations in life, but the greatest of them all is to be invited by God into His Kingdom: being put to death in the flesh but quickened by the Spirit." By that Spirit he preached even to those in prison, proving again that He descended to the depths but was not abandoned there. And when He died, the centurion had a revelation, the earth shook, graves were opened, and many saints arose. For those who die in righteousness, there is no waiting in limbo; they are immediately with the Lord. Elijah was taken up in a chariot. Enoch was translated, not seeing death, because he pleased God. The thief on the cross said, "Lord, remember me," and Jesus replied, "Today shalt thou be with me in paradise."

That is the right expectation. For in the days of Noah, eight souls were saved by water, and now Christ is our ark of safety. In Him we are protected from all that stands against the will of God. As Paul stated, "I can do all things through Christ who strengthens me." Not all things in general, but all things within God's will that lead to a godly life. Baptism itself is not the washing of the body but the pledge of a good conscience toward God through the resurrection of Jesus Christ.

With the heart one believes to righteousness, and with the mouth confession is made to salvation. Now He is ascended into heaven, seated at the right hand of God, with angels, authorities, and powers made subject to Him. When our ways align with God's means, the result is life in Christ.

There is no comparison to God. He is above all, and everything else lies beneath him.